NEW VANGUARD 252

M113 APC 1960–75

US, ARVN, and Australian variants in Vietnam

JAMIE PRENATT ILLUSTRATED BY HENRY MORSHEAD
& JOHNNY SHUMATE

OSPREY PUBLISHING
Bloomsbury Publishing Plc

Kemp House, Chawley Park, Cumnor Hill, Oxford OX2 9PH, UK
29 Earlsfort Terrace, Dublin 2, Ireland
1385 Broadway, 5th Floor, New York, NY 10018, USA
Email: info@ospreypublishing.com
www.ospreypublishing.com

OSPREY is a trademark of Osprey Publishing Ltd

First published in Great Britain in 2017
Transferred to digital print in 2024

© Osprey Publishing Ltd, 2017

All rights reserved. No part of this publication may be used or reproduced in any form without the prior written permission, except in the case of brief quotations embodied in critical articles or reviews. Inquiries should be addressed to the Publisher.

A catalog record for this book is available from the British Library.

Print ISBN: 978 1 4728 1746 4
ePub: 978 1 4728 1748 8
ePDF: 978 1 4728 1747 1
XML: 978 1 4728 2647 3

Index by Sandra Shotter
Typeset in Sabon and Myriad Pro
Page layouts by PDQ Digital Media Solutions, Bungay, UK
Printed and bound in India by Replika Press Private Ltd.

24 25 26 27 28   10 9 8 7 6 5

The Woodland Trust
Osprey Publishing supports the Woodland Trust, the UK's leading woodland conservation charity.

www.ospreypublishing.com
To find out more about our authors and books visit our website. Here you will find extracts, author interviews, details of forthcoming events and the option to sign-up for our newsletter.

Cover image
A column of Armored Cavalry Assault Vehicles (ACAVs), one of the conflict's iconic weapons, on patrol. (DoD)

CONTENTS

INTRODUCTION 4
- The progenitors

DESIGN AND DEVELOPMENT 8
- The M113

MAJOR VARIANTS 9
- M113 ACAV
- M125 and M106
- M577
- M132
- M548
- XM163
- XM734
- XM806E1
- M113A1 Fire Support Vehicle (FSV)
- M113A1 Fitter's vehicle

COMBAT HISTORY: SOUTH VIETNAM 18
- Ap Bac – January 2, 1963
- Duc Co – August 9, 1965
- Operations in Cambodia – April–June 1970
- Lam Son 719 – February–March 1971

COMBAT HISTORY: UNITED STATES 28
- Ap Bau Bang – November 11, 1965 and March 19–20, 1967
- Ambush at Ap Hung Nghia – November 21, 1966
- The second battle of Suoi Cat – May 21, 1967
- The anonymous battle – March 26, 1970

COMBAT HISTORY: AUSTRALIA 37
- The battle of Long Tan – August 18, 1966
- Operation *Hammersley* – February–March 1970

OTHER FREE-WORLD FORCES 45
- South Korea
- Thailand
- Philippines

SELECTED BIBLIOGRAPHY 47

INDEX 48

M113 APC 1960–75

US, ARVN, AND AUSTRALIAN VARIANTS IN VIETNAM

INTRODUCTION

The M113 is one of the most numerous, widely deployed, and adaptable armored vehicles ever produced. Approximately 85,000 were manufactured and they served in over 50 countries. Remarkably for an armored vehicle designed over 55 years ago, many still remain in service in the US Army and worldwide. Although slated to be replaced by the Armored Multi-Purpose Vehicle at the brigade level and below in the US Army, this process will likely not be complete before the late 2020s and there are approximately 1,900 more M113s requiring replacement above brigade level. The M113's longevity is a testimony to the soundness of the original design and its flexibility.

Although the M113 would later see combat service elsewhere, the war in Vietnam represented both its combat debut and its most challenging operational environment. The US Army initially believed that Vietnam was unsuitable for armor operations and did not support sending armored vehicles there, either its own or those of its allies. Not only did the M113 play a key role in refuting this notion, its mobility and firepower would often prove to be tactically decisive.

The progenitors
The development of a tracked, fully enclosed armored personnel carrier (APC) began in late 1944. It was intended to address some of the M3 half-track's shortcomings, including the vulnerability that resulted from thin armor and the lack of overhead protection and its limited cross-country mobility compared to fully tracked vehicles.

Designated the T13 armored utility vehicle, the concept design had a box-shaped hull and used the powertrain and suspension components of the M24 Chaffee light tank that entered production that same year. Its projected maximum road speed would have made it only slightly slower than the M3 half-track, but it would have carried armor twice as thick. The project never progressed beyond the concept stage and was canceled in early 1945 after it was determined that the T13 would be underpowered.

Shortly after, work began on a new design using the powertrain of the M18 Hellcat tank destroyer. The T16 armored utility vehicle was similar in configuration to the T13, but larger. There was a crew of three: driver, bow machine-gunner, and commander. There was room in the rear of the hull

The M44 (T16) undergoing evaluation. It was armed with a .50-caliber machine gun at the rear of the hull roof and a bow-mounted .30-caliber machine gun. The latter weapon could be relocated to one of several socket mounts on the roof as shown here. (DoD)

for 24 infantry, seated on four benches; two along each side of the interior and two arranged back-to-back in the center of the hull. Access was via two large doors in the rear of the hull. On each side, there were four firing ports with sliding shutters and an escape hatch. It was standardized as the M44 armored utility vehicle, but did not enter series production as its size made it unsuitable as a squad-sized armored personnel carrier.

To meet the existing requirement for a fully tracked, squad-sized personnel carrier development of the T18 armored utility vehicle began in the fall of 1946. It was based on the chassis of the T43E1 cargo tractor, originally intended as a prime mover for 155mm and lighter artillery pieces. The pilot vehicles differed in configuration and armament. The definitive version was the T18E1, standardized as the M75. Production began in 1952 and almost 1,800 were manufactured by International Harvester and the Food Machinery and Chemical Corporation (later renamed the FMC Corporation) before production ended in 1954.

The driver's station was at the front left corner of the vehicle and the engine was to his right. In the center of the vehicle and immediately behind the engine was a low cupola for the commander that mounted a .50-caliber machine gun. There were two roof hatches and two doors for access in the

The M75 was the first US armored personnel carrier to enter full production after World War II. The similarity to the later M113 in configuration is clearly evident in this view. The vehicle's high cost led to it being superseded by the M59. (DoD)

A late-production M59 with the M13 commander's cupola. Although it met the goal of being less expensive than the M75 – it was only one-third of the cost – the M59 was underpowered and its cruising range was inadequate. The raised area on the hull roofline is the location of one of the engine's air intake and exhaust grills. (DoD)

rear of the hull. Development began on mortar carrier versions, but these did not enter production. The M75 saw action in the latter stages of the Korean War where it demonstrated its usefulness in a number of roles.

The M75's high cost led to a program to develop a less expensive alternative even before the first M75s left the production line. The six FMC-designed and manufactured T59 pilot vehicles shared the same basic layout with the driver and commander at the front of the vehicle and two engines and transmissions, one in each of the left and right hull sides. A ramp formed the rear of the hull, greatly improving access. Later, an escape door would be incorporated into the ramp. The vehicle was also amphibious, being propelled in the water by its tracks, and fitted with a trim vane at the front of the hull. The commander had a low-profile cupola and pintle-mounted .50-caliber machine gun, although this was replaced on later production examples with the M13 cupola that permitted the commander to load, aim, and fire the machine gun while under armor protection. It was standardized as the M59 and more than 6,300 were produced between 1953 and 1960. A 4.2-inch mortar carrier variant, the M84, entered service in 1955.

A

1: An ARVN (Army of the Republic of Vietnam) M113 with an armored shield for the .50-caliber machine gun, introduced after the loss of numerous crewman at the battle of Ap Bac. This was the "standard" configuration, although ARVN M113s often mounted one or more side-mounted machine guns as well. The vehicle here retains its shrouds over the tracks; these were almost always removed on US M113s to prevent the buildup of mud and vegetation.

2: An M113 ACAV fitted with the Type A armor kit belonging to the 4th Infantry Division's 1st Squadron/10th Cavalry in 1971. The Squadron's vehicle markings were distinctive, consisting of a large cavalry guidon and vehicle number painted on the sides. The vehicle here is fitted with the belly armor kit. The armor extended only as far back as the rear of the engine compartment and provided no protection for the vehicle's passenger compartment. The concentration of the extra weight under the front of the vehicle increased wear on the drive train and unbalanced the vehicle while swimming. To correct the latter problem, high floatation trim vanes were fitted on the front as shown here.

3: The XM734. Developed as an interim measure pending the development of a purpose-built infantry fighting vehicle for the US Army, a number were sent to South Vietnam for operational testing where they served with both US and ARVN forces. The vehicle commander's station on the US XM734s received the Okinawa pattern armor kit as shown here, while at least one of the ARVN vehicles was fitted with the M74C turret.

The original T113 prototype. It can be easily distinguished as the T113's blunt nose and trailing idler wheel were replaced with a larger sloping glacis plate and raised idler wheel on the T113E2, which would be standardized as the M113 in April 1959. (DoD)

DESIGN AND DEVELOPMENT

The T113 emerged from a 1954 US Army requirement for an air-droppable, multi-purpose family of vehicles based on a common chassis and built around two armored carriers, one with a weight of 16,000lb and the other of 8,000lb. Proposals for wheeled vehicles were quickly discarded due to their inadequate cross-country mobility. The heavier of the two carriers addressed the need for a tracked personnel carrier capable of transporting an infantry squad. The lighter one (the T114, later standardized as the M114) was a command and reconnaissance vehicle. The FMC Corporation received a contract for the production of 16 pilot vehicles, including ten personnel carriers, two 81mm mortar carriers, three Dart antitank missile carriers, and one chassis that could be used as the basis for other trials. In 1957, FMC produced two versions of the personnel carrier. The T113 featured new aluminum alloy armor and the externally similar but heavier T117 used conventional steel armor.

Later that same year, the requirements for the personnel carrier changed. The most important of these changes was for a vehicle with increased armor protection. The new requirements called for an air-droppable version of no more than 17,500lb and a second version with armor protection at least as great as the M59 and a maximum weight of 24,000lb. These two versions were designated T113E1 and T113E2 respectively. Testing revealed that with a minor weight reduction of 400lb the T113E2 could fulfill both requirements. This was achieved, in part, by reducing the thickness of the floor and the underside of the sponsons. Operational experience in Vietnam would later show the need for reinforcement of both areas.

The M113

The M113 armored personnel carrier had a box-shaped hull with a relatively low silhouette. It had excellent mobility and was amphibious. For operation in the water, a plywood trim vane on the vehicle's glacis would be extended. Shrouds to improve performance in the water covered the top of the vehicle's running gear, but these were almost universally removed in Vietnam as they were easily damaged, collected debris, and made field repairs to the track and suspension components more time consuming.

The driver's position was located at the front left corner of the hull. His instrument cluster was to his left and there was a small bank of indicator lights to his immediate front. The driver controlled the vehicle using two differential steering levers; later two pivot steering levers were added for short radius turns and while the vehicle was in the water. The seat was adjustable and four periscopes provided vision when the vehicle was "buttoned up;" an additional infrared periscope could also be fitted in the driver's hatch. In Vietnam, drivers normally operated with their heads exposed due to the heat and the much better visibility possible in that position.

To the right of the driver was the engine and transmission. The engine originally fitted was the gasoline-powered 212hp Chrysler Model 75 V8. In mid-1959, evaluation began of a new transmission and commercial diesel engine. After trials, the General Motors 6V53 diesel was selected. Most importantly, the use of the diesel power plant reduced the risk of fire, but it also improved fuel economy and thus cruising range. In addition to the new engine and transmission, the fuel tank capacity was increased from 80 to 95 gallons. This improved vehicle was standardized as the M113A1 and entered full-scale production in 1964.

The M113A1 armored personnel carrier. It had excellent mobility, could be adapted to a wide variety of roles, and provided adequate protection from small arms fire. Designed as a "battlefield taxi" to deliver infantry safely to the point at which they could dismount, the operational environment in Vietnam led them to be used in new ways. It was armed with a single .50-caliber machine gun on an exposed pintle mount that left the commander vulnerable when employing it. (DoD)

Immediately behind the engine and centered in the hull was the commander's position. He had an adjustable seat, a small, manually rotating cupola fitted with five periscopes, and an external mount for a .50-caliber machine gun. Commanders invariably operated standing in their position. This led to unacceptable losses in action and both improvised armor and, later, standardized armor kits were fitted to reduce their vulnerability.

The M113/M113A1 was designed to carry 11 infantry, ten seated on folding benches along each side and one on a folding jump seat directly behind the commander's seat. There was a large hatch above the troop compartment that allowed a few of the passengers to fight while mounted. Mounted on the interior hull wall at the upper left rear of the troop compartment was the fuel tank.

A hydraulically operated ramp that formed nearly the entire back of the hull provided easy access to the interior. It was fitted with a door for dismounting when the vehicle was under artillery or mortar fire.

MAJOR VARIANTS

From the outset, the M113 chassis was envisioned as the basis for a family of vehicles performing a wide variety of roles. These included mortar carrier, resupply, command and control, medical evacuation, air defense, anti-tank and ballistic missile launchers, and missile support vehicles. Many of these served in Vietnam. In addition, the versatility of the M113 series and combat experience in Vietnam led to it being used for other roles as well.

Variants using the M113A1 typically also carried the "A1" suffix (e.g. M125A1).

M113 ACAV

High casualties among vehicle commanders during the M113's early engagements prompted the development of armor to provide the necessary protection. Initially these were simple, locally fabricated shields that provided protection mainly to the front. Later,

An M113 equipped with FMC's "A" kit, which supplanted the early locally and theater-produced armor protection solutions. On the roof to the right of the vehicle commander's station is stored the tripod for the .50-caliber machine gun for use in a dismounted role. (DoD)

The M106 can be distinguished from the otherwise externally similar M125 by the presence of the large bridge assembly and baseplate stored on the left side of the vehicle and the rotator assembly stored on the left rear mudguard, components used when the mortar was fired dismounted from the vehicle. On the right, a gunner "hangs" a 4.2-inch mortar round just before firing. (LEFT: DoD / RIGHT: NARA)

a standardized armor package of flat armor plates that provided all-round protection was produced in Okinawa. In 1966 FMC began producing a new armor protection system. The "A" kit consisted of a forward shield and two curved side pieces for the commander; as with the Okinawa kit, the commander's open hatch provided protection from the rear. It also included shields for two M60 machine guns mounted on the roof and manned by gunners standing in the troop compartment. The "B" kit, consisting of the commander's armor only, was used on the M125 and M106 mortar carriers.

M113s mounting the "A" kit were colloquially known as ACAVs – Armored Cavalry Assault Vehicles – as cavalry units used their M113s with "A" kits more as light tanks than armored personnel carriers.

M125 and M106
Self-propelled carriers for the 81mm and 4.2-inch mortar were envisioned from the beginning of the M113's development. Entering service in 1964 as the M125 and M106 respectively, they had a large circular split hatch in the troop compartment roof that provided an opening through which the mortar, mounted on a turntable, could fire. The M125 carried 114 rounds of ammunition, while the M106 carried 93 (88 in the M106A1) of the larger 4.2-inch projectiles.

B

1: An M132 belonging to B Company, 15th Combat Engineer Battalion. Unlike almost all other M113-series vehicles, this one carries a two-color camouflage paint pattern. Despite the vulnerability resulting from the thin armor and large flamethrower fuel tanks in the passenger compartment, their psychological effect on the enemy was profound and they could reduce even the most heavily fortified positions. They were also frequently used for the more pedestrian task of burning away vegetation. Their most limiting characteristic from an operational perspective was their short firing time, about 30 seconds, after which they had to be refueled in a protected area.

2: The M106 4.2-inch mortar carrier. As can be seen here, when the mortar was not being used dismounted, its bridge assembly and baseplate were normally carried on the left side of the vehicle. In US armored cavalry troops, each platoon was authorized a single M106; these were normally consolidated at the troop level where they could be used more flexibly and with greater effect.

3: Although there were numerous attempts to increase the firepower of the M113, one of the more common was the installation of a 106mm recoilless rifle. They typically served with the ARVN, being organic to the armored cavalry troop, but also saw limited service with US units as well. The recoilless rifles were invariably mounted on the right side of the vehicle.

1

2

3

The US, ARVN, and Australian forces operated the M577, here (right) towing a trailer as it moves along a muddy road. The raised box-like structure to the right of the driver contains a generator. It carries two rolls of concertina wire on the front of the hull and the trailer has spacers to enable the tires to follow in the path of the M577's tracks as a preventative measure against mines. The 11th Armored Cavalry Regiment's Tactical Operations Center (below) at Lai Khe, showing M577s with the tents erected, one for each of the four primary headquarters staff sections. The curved pipe-like device on the roof is a lifting davit that, when fitted into brackets on the front of the raised hull section, could be used to dismount the generator. (NARA)

M577

Another early variant was the M577. Developed in response to a need for a command post vehicle, the most distinctive feature was the troop compartment's raised hull section. It was fitted with a folding table along the left wall, racks for additional radios, and carried an externally mounted generator. It also had a large tent that could be extended from the rear of the vehicle to provide additional working space. M577s were assigned to battalion/squadron, brigade, and division headquarters elements where they served as the tactical operations center, fire direction center, and medical aid station.

M132

Development of a mechanized flamethrower began in 1954. The resulting unit was installed for evaluation purposes in the M59, but as the M113 was just coming into service, the M113 was chosen to mount the new system. Designated M132 and popularly known in Vietnam as the "Zippo track," it had a crew of two: driver and commander/gunner. An M8 cupola mounting the flame gun and a coaxial 7.62mm machine gun replaced the M113's commander's cupola and the M10 fuel and pressure unit occupied the entire passenger compartment. The 200-gallon fuel supply for the flamethrower allowed for 32 seconds of firing. The range of the flamethrower was 11m–200m (35–650ft). A total of 351 M132s and M132A1s were produced.

The M10 fuel and pressure unit (far left) consisted of four fuel tanks containing gasoline and a thickening agent and four smaller compressed air tanks, two of each being visible here, as well as the associated piping. An M132A1 in action (left) during Operation *Cedar Falls* being used to burn away vegetation and clear antipersonnel mines. Given its thin armor and limited flamethrower fuel supply it required selective use. It did, however, have a devastating effect on enemy morale and was very effective against personnel in dense vegetation or bunkers and other field fortifications. A single M132 was organic to the headquarters companies of US armored and cavalry units. Some South Vietnamese armor regiments each had four. M132s were sometimes also carried aboard Armored Troop Carriers (ATCs) of the riverine fleet prior to the installation of M8 cupolas on riverine fleet vessels. (FAR LEFT: DoD / LEFT: NARA)

M548

The M548 was an unarmored cargo carrier capable of carrying 6 tons, originally intended to provide ammunition resupply for self-propelled artillery. In Vietnam, it was also pressed into service to resupply armored formations and land-clearing teams in the field that were inaccessible to wheeled transport. M548s were also modified to provide support to mechanized flamethrowers in the field. They were fitted with cab and hull armor and carried flamethrower fuel storage tanks, a mixing tank, an air compressor, and connections to transfer both the thickened fuel and air. These were designated XM45E1.

The South Vietnamese employed some M548s fitted with ramps to carry 105mm towed howitzers that could be quickly dismounted for firing, giving them a degree of mobility almost equal to that of self-propelled artillery.

XM163

Although there was no enemy air threat over South Vietnam, three battalions equipped with the M42 Duster served there where they provided useful service in the ground support role, particularly providing perimeter defense and convoy escort. However, the M42 was obsolescent as an air defense weapon and an effort to replace it had been underway since 1952.

The system adopted, later standardized as the M163 – also known as the Vulcan Air Defense System – began production in 1967. It consisted of a turret-mounted 20mm Gatling-type cannon on an M113A1 modified with a suspension-locking device to provide a more stable firing platform (the gun mount was later modified, resulting in the M163A1). Floatation cells on the side and high displacement trim vane compensated for the added weight of the gun, turret, and ammunition when swimming. The gunner could select a rate of fire of either 1,000 or 3,000 rounds per minute, the high rate having a burst limiter to conserve ammunition.

In November 1968 the 1st Vulcan Combat Team (Provisional) began a 120-day evaluation period in the II Field Force Vietnam area of

With mobility comparable to the M113, the M548 was vital to sustaining armor in the field, where wheeled logistics vehicles were unable to go. Here Vietnamese civilians look on as two M548s wait for their turn to ford a river while an M110 howitzer begins to cross. (NARA)

XM163 Vulcans in Vietnam. Special equipment fitted for their evaluation in a ground support role included a telescopic sight and night vision equipment. As shown above, most of the XM163s operated without their range-only radar fitted as it was superfluous given the lack of an enemy air threat. Above right, an XM163 fires while on a search and destroy mission. (NARA)

responsibility to determine the XM163's suitability for combat in Vietnam. It consisted of five XM163s (including one maintenance float) operating in sections of two. They performed many of the same missions as the M42, including, in order of frequency, perimeter defense, security for engineer minesweeping operations, convoy security, and reconnaissance in force operations. They also performed ambushes, security for medical civic action and engineer quarry/soil operations, and show of force missions. During these operations they engaged a total of 110 targets, often at ranges as short as 25m (82ft). The XM163s performed well and were highly valued for their firepower and the mobility that allowed them to keep pace with the ACAVs they supported in combat. Their tour was extended by 45 days to meet operational requirements associated with the Tet counteroffensive.

XM734

Another variant sent to Vietnam in small numbers for evaluation purposes was the XM734 Mechanized Infantry Combat Vehicle. This was an interim design intended as a stopgap pending the development of a purpose-built infantry fighting vehicle. It was fitted with four vision blocks and firing ports in each side and two in the rear ramp. The bench seats were relocated to the center of the troop compartment to allow the passengers to face outwards.

XM806E1

A recovery variant of the M113A1, the XM806E1 had a 20,000lb winch in the passenger compartment and a 3,000lb capacity crane that could be erected on the roof. XM806E1s served in very small numbers; one was

The XM734 moves through a rice paddy with M113s. Photos of it in the field invariably show troops riding on top of the vehicle or standing in the open top passenger compartment hatch. This was due to the heat, danger from mines, and the superior visibility it afforded. Unlike the prototype that mounted the M74C turret with twin .30-caliber machine guns, US XM734s in Vietnam all appear to have single .50-caliber machine guns on pintle mounts protected by the Okinawa-style armor kits. (NARA)

The XM803E1. The most prominent visual feature was the stabilizing spade mounted on each of the hull's rear corners which were lowered to provide additional purchase during winching operations. (NARA)

photographed with the 1st Battalion/61st Infantry Regiment, 5th Infantry Division (Mechanized) and another in ARVN service in 1971.

M113A1 Fire Support Vehicle (FSV)

The Australian M113A1 was the only vehicle of its type to serve in Vietnam. Designed as an interim solution to the requirement for an air-portable armored fighting vehicle, 15 M113A1s were fitted with the turret of a Saladin armored car, which became available when the Australian Army converted from wheeled to tracked armored vehicles. The M113A1 was armed with a 76mm cannon and two .30-caliber machine guns, one mounted coaxially to the main gun and the other on the turret roof.

The conversion involved installation of a new roof section with a raised turret ring and racks for 76mm ammunition and the removal of the personnel compartment benches. As with the XM163, the weight of the turret reduced the FSV's freeboard while swimming and the vehicle was given an enlarged trim vane and a screen that could be raised around the engine's air intake.

Evaluation trials that began in 1967 took almost three years and the first FSVs did not arrive in Vietnam until mid-1971.

The crew of an FSV from A Squadron, 3rd Cavalry Regiment takes a break (below left) while escorting a column of 5-ton trucks towing M2A2 howitzers. Note that in addition to the more obvious modifications, the driver's hatch was replaced with one that swung to the side in order to avoid interfering with the turret's traverse. All the FSVs in South Vietnam were fitted with reinforcement plates under the sponsons and belly armor to protect against mines and, like the tanks, had their turret-mounted smoke grenade dischargers removed as they were inevitably damaged as the vehicles moved through heavy vegetation. An interior view (below) shows the turret basket and ammunition storage in racks on hull walls and bins on the hull floor. (BELOW LEFT: Australian War Memorial P02675.023 / BELOW RIGHT: CC-BY-SA Jp-8000)

The M113A1 Fitter's vehicle was used by a variety of RAEME units including the 106th and 102nd Field Workshops, 17 Construction Squadron, 1st Field Squadron and the Light Aid Detachments supporting the M113A1 and Centurion-equipped squadrons. In the latter role, they provided the constant repair and routine maintenance necessary to sustain armored operations in the field. They closely accompanied the combat units and, being armed, saw combat on a number of occasions. (Australian War Memorial P12609.006)

M113A1 Fitter's vehicle

Another M113A1 variant used only by Australia in Vietnam was the Fitter's vehicle.

This was a repair vehicle manned by the craftsmen of the Royal Australian Electrical and Mechanical Engineers (RAEME). It had an enlarged roof hatch, a hydraulic crane with a capacity of 6,800lb that was operated from the driver's station, and carried the tools and parts necessary to repair tanks and other armored vehicles. The large roof hatch that opened to the right enabled large components such as engines and transmissions to be carried internally.

C

1: This Australian M113A1 has olive drab paint that replaced the khaki color of the first armored vehicles deployed to South Vietnam. It has the Cadillac Gage T50 turret, designed to provide the vehicle commander with increased protection. Due to the turret's slow traverse and other problems, a .30-caliber machine gun was often removed from the turret and mounted externally. This enabled fleeting targets to be engaged, but at the cost of losing the all-round armor protection that the turret was designed to provide. The red square marking on the sides identifies it as being from B Squadron, 3rd Cavalry Regiment. Nicknamed "Blood," it was the section commander's vehicle; the other two M113A1s in the section were nicknamed "Sweat" and "Tears" after the musical group Blood, Sweat & Tears.

2: An M113A1 Fitter's vehicle belonging to 17 Construction Squadron. It is armed with the .50-caliber machine gun with supplemental armored shield, a necessity given that the Fitter's vehicles normally closely accompanied armored units in the field and occasionally participated in combat. The shield, with its slightly different shape and sharp corners, is not the later standard pattern and may have been fabricated locally by the unit. The marking "Bushie's Bluebell Mk II" reflects the radio designation given to RAEME units and the nickname of RAEME craftsmen ("bluebells").

3: This M113A1 Fire Support Vehicle nicknamed "The Sandgroper" carries the blue triangle marking of A Squadron, 3rd Cavalry Regiment. Its call sign – 42 – lacks a letter suffix, indicating it is the section commander's vehicle. Other M113A1 FSVs carried the nicknames "Belinda," "Bewitched," "Bothered," "Bewildered," and "Denise" on their sides. One had the nickname "Camalco" painted on its barrel, a reference to a large Australian aluminum company and the M113's aluminum armor. The FSVs were colloquially referred to as "beasts," a name that sometimes was carried in addition to the vehicle nickname. The smoke grenade launchers on the turret have been removed and the mounting plate is bronze green, the original color of the Saladin armored cars from which the turrets had been removed.

1

2

3

COMBAT HISTORY: SOUTH VIETNAM

ABOVE AND BELOW
ARVN M113s in the field. The lack of armor protection for the gunner manning the .50-caliber machine gun resulted in high casualties at the battle of Ap Bac. The South Vietnamese had previously identified the need for such protection, but the change had not been approved prior to the battle. Shields were quickly fabricated to remedy this shortcoming and were a standard fit to all ARVN M113s fielded beginning in 1964. (NARA)

The combat history of the M113 begins with the transfer of 32 M113s to the Army of the Republic of Vietnam (ARVN) in April of 1962 to evaluate the combat capabilities of the then-new vehicle in an operational setting. They were organized into two mechanized companies, the 7th and 21st (sharing the numerical designations of the infantry divisions to which they were attached), each consisting of a headquarters platoon with two M113s, three rifle platoons each with three M113s, and a support platoon equipped with four M113s (three carrying 60mm mortars and the fourth a 3.5in rocket launcher). They were assigned to the IV Corps Tactical Zone (CTZ) in the southernmost part of Vietnam, not an ideal area for armor operations given its dominant geographic features were the Mekong Delta, canals, swamps, and other water obstacles.

Despite the poor terrain, the M113's mobility and shock effect resulted in a number of very successful engagements throughout 1962. Most notably in late September the 7th Company, during operations in the Plain of Reeds, routed the 502nd Battalion, killed 150 main force Viet Cong (VC) and captured 38 prisoners and 27 weapons. Most significantly, this action demonstrated the value of using the M113 as an assault vehicle, rather than simply as a means to transport infantry who would dismount near their objective as called for by US doctrine.

In late 1962, the 7th and 21st companies were reorganized into 4th and 5th armored cavalry troops subordinate to armor regiments (designated armored cavalry squadrons in 1967). They had a similar organization to the mechanized companies but with 81mm mortars and a 57mm recoilless rifle replacing the 60mm

mortars and 3.5in rocket launcher respectively. The number of troops was increased to six and their operating area expanded to include all four CTZs.

As the South Vietnamese received more M113s, the number of armored cavalry troops grew and by early 1966 the ARVN fielded 24. In the late 1960s, the Table of Organization and Equipment for the armored cavalry troops changed again. The three platoons grew from three to five M113s APCs and there was an M113 mounting a 106mm recoilless rifle, and a platoon of M125 81mm mortar carriers was added for a total of 22 M113-based vehicles. Armored cavalry squadrons consisted of a tank troop and two M113 troops; the squadron headquarters included one M106 self-propelled mortar and a platoon of M132 flamethrowers. A single squadron was assigned at the infantry division and corps level. Each armor brigade had two or more squadrons.

South Vietnamese armor operations tended to be of short duration and for limited objectives. This was largely due to the lack of a robust logistics system that would have enabled extended operations.

Ap Bac – January 2, 1963

The battle of Ap Bac overshadowed the early successes. The 4th Troop was part of an ARVN 7th Infantry Division operation designed to capture a radio transmitter located in the hamlet of Ap Tah Thot, located 1.5km (about 1 mile) from Ap Bac and 65km (about 40 miles) southwest of Saigon. The transmitter was protected by what was reported to be a reinforced company-sized enemy force and the objective was located in an area of flooded rice paddies, irrigation ditches, and canals. The plan was to insert an infantry battalion north of the hamlet by helicopter that would then conduct an assault to destroy the transmitter and enemy force. Two Civil Guard battalions would advance from the south. The 4th Troop was moving on a course west of and parallel to the Civil Guard battalions.

The plan went awry from the start. The enemy force was more than three times larger than that which had been reported and the northern force inserted by helicopter was pinned down by heavy fire. One of the Civil Guard battalions was ambushed and the battalion commander, one of the company commanders, and 20 troops became casualties, after which both battalions were ordered to assume blocking positions. Reinforcements in the form of an infantry company were landed by helicopter 300m (985ft) west of enemy positions in Ap Bac. Of the 15 helicopters used to attempt to land the company, 14 were hit, four were shot down, and one was forced down due to mechanical failure. The 4th Troop, which was advancing from the west, was ordered to come to the aid of the downed aircrew, but was delayed for several hours as it attempted to cross a number of canals with particularly steep banks. The last crossing involved filling the canal with brush and using each M113 to assist the following vehicle out of the canal using tow cables. Every two M113s that crossed moved toward the objective as a pair, rather than waiting to reorganize. The assault was made by six of the Troop's M113s. As the Troop moved toward Ap Bac and deployed from column to line formation, the VC opened fire at short range. The Troop's advance stalled after two of the Troop's officers were killed and six of the exposed gunners manning the .50-caliber machine guns became casualties. About 15 percent of the Troop became incapacitated, including four personnel in one of the Troop's command vehicles. Further reinforcements in the form of

An assault bridge mounted on an M113 is demonstrated at the South Vietnamese Armor School. Although the M113 possessed a high degree of mobility, water obstacles and ditches with steep banks posed a particular problem and the South Vietnamese produced 24 of the M113-mounted aluminum balk bridges. (NARA)

two companies of paratroops were dropped that evening just before dusk and a second armored cavalry troop also arrived. When the attack resumed the next morning, the ARVN found that the VC had withdrawn during the night.

From the perspective of M113 employment, the battle underscored an important need: armor protection for the vehicle commander operating the .50-caliber machine gun. Shields would become widely used and the ARVN also adopted the M74, a purpose-built turret equipped with two .30-caliber machine guns.

Duc Co – August 9, 1965

The Duc Co Special Forces Camp, 40km (25 miles) west of Pleiku, had been surrounded by the North Vietnamese Army (NVA) 32nd Regiment for over a month and several ARVN attempts to relieve it had failed. In early August, the 32nd Regiment increased its pressure on the camp and established a two-battalion ambush along a 6km (3.5-mile) stretch of highway leading to the camp. In response to the increased enemy activity, a task force consisting of elements of the 3rd Armored Regiment headquarters, two troops of M41 tanks, a troop of M113s, the 21st Ranger Group, an engineer company, and a battery of 105mm howitzers was formed to relieve the camp.

The enemy's tactic of establishing ambushes to engage relief forces was well known and, when the ARVN column entered the kill zone and triggered the ambush, it immediately charged the main body of attackers and called in air support. The two-hour action caused the NVA to withdraw. Operations around Duc Co in August resulted in over 560 enemy killed and 26 captured, as well as the capture of over 100 individual and crew-served weapons.

D

1: A South Vietnamese M113 with M74 turret assigned to an unknown unit in Quang Ngai province. The M74's cramped confines were apparently not an issue for the small-statured Vietnamese and the turrets were fitted to numerous vehicles. While the two .30-caliber machine guns had a higher rate of fire than the .50-caliber, they lacked the penetrating power of the larger weapon.

2: The South Korean M113s of the Capital Division were among the most vividly painted of the war, with a three-color camouflage pattern and a large tiger head insignia carried on the front that reflected the Division's "Tiger" nickname. This one carries a non-standard armor kit for the vehicle commander's station and side-mounted M60 7.62mm machine gun.

3: Like the M113s of the Capital Division, those of the South Korean 9th Infantry Division also carried large markings reflecting their unit nickname, "White Horse." This vehicle is a standard M113 equipped with a single .50-caliber machine gun. Like other Korean M113s in Vietnam, it also retains its track shrouds.

Operations in Cambodia – April–June 1970

The incursions into Cambodia were the largest and most complex armored operations undertaken by the ARVN. The ARVN forces included nine armored cavalry squadrons, about half of the ARVN's armor. During the Cambodian incursions, the ARVN performed well and, in the initial stages, operations were executed without US advisors. Aided by good weather and favorable terrain, ARVN armor was aggressively led. It inflicted heavy losses on the NVA and VC forces that used the border for rest and reorganization and severely disrupted their logistical infrastructure, including the capture of large qualities of weapons, food, ammunition, and other stores.

Toan Thang 41

On April 14, three task forces, each consisting of an armored cavalry squadron and two or three battalions of infantry under the control of III Corps, launched the initial cross-border operation into the region known as the Parrot's Beak. Lasting three days, the operation resulted in over 400 enemy killed or captured and the seizure of 100 weapons and 200 tons of rice. Despite some coordination problems between the armor and infantry, ARVN casualties were light, with only eight killed and 67 wounded.

Toan Thang 42

The first phase of this operation into the Parrot's Beak began on April 28 and was similar to Toan Thang 41 in terms of the task organization of the ARVN forces. Not having the benefit of surprise, it encountered resistance early, but the ARVN armor used maneuver and shock effect and the task forces were able to overcome most resistance without having to rely on supporting artillery or air assets.

The second phase was intended to destroy enemy forces in the Ba Thu Secret Zone (Base Area 367). This large operation involved the three III Corps task forces and major elements of the IV Corps, including five armored cavalry squadrons, the 9th Infantry Division, and a regiment-sized ranger group. The III Corps task forces attacked to the west and south, while the IV Corps units – organized in four armor-infantry task forces – moved up from the south. It resulted in over 1,200 enemy killed or captured, along with the seizure of 1,000 individual and 60 crew-served weapons for the loss of 66 killed and 330 wounded.

A column of ARVN M113s. The first and third vehicles have the standard ARVN shield for the .50-caliber machine gun, while the second has been fitted with the M74C turret. Typically, they also carry a side-mounted .30-caliber machine gun. Note also the sections of aluminum balk carried along the side, used to assist in recovering mired vehicles. (NARA)

The remaining three phases of the operation were similar in nature and results.

Cuu Long/SD 9/06
This was a 6km (3.5-mile) advance into the Crow's Nest on April 20 conducted by an armored cavalry squadron and elements of the 9th Infantry Division. The ARVN forces overcame determined resistance, killing 171 enemy and capturing a storage depot containing over 1,000 weapons and a large quantity of ammunition. Again, ARVN casualties were relatively modest: 24 killed and 111 wounded.

Lam Son 719 – February–March 1971
Conceived by the US, Lam Son 719 was an incursion into southeastern Laos. The intent was to interdict the Ho Chi Minh Trail and destroy supplies being stockpiled in the vicinity of Tchepone with the objective of disrupting an expected NVA offensive and facilitating the withdrawal of US forces from Vietnam. Unlike the Cambodian incursion, no US ground forces would cross the border, but the plan depended heavily on US air support. The plan entailed a series of heliborne operations to seize intermediate objectives and establish firebases as well as a ground thrust along Route 9. The latter move would be conducted by a force composed primarily of the two armored cavalry squadrons – the 11th and 17th – of the 1st Armored Brigade and the three infantry battalions of the 1st Airborne Brigade. Route 9, the only east–west road in the area, was a single-lane road in very poor repair, bordered by thick vegetation on both sides and dominated by high ground to the north. Three ARVN Ranger battalions would establish firebases parallel to and north of Route 9 while two regiments of the 1st Infantry Division did the same to the south. Enemy forces, originally estimated at three infantry regiments, would ultimately grow to five infantry divisions, supported by armor, long-range artillery, and approximately 20 battalions of antiaircraft artillery.

ARVN forces crossed the border on February 8. Although initial enemy resistance was light, the ground force was delayed by extensive damage to Route 9 and the dense jungle along the sides of the road. The ground force linked up with a heliborne force at Landing Zone A Loui on February 10, where one M113 was lost and another damaged during subsequent reconnaissance operations in the surrounding area. By the 16th, the advance had stalled and the South Vietnamese forces came under heavy attack, including by T-54 and PT-76 tanks. A task force composed of the 17th Armored Squadron and two airborne companies moved north from A Loui to relieve heavy enemy pressure on the nearby Fire Support Base 31, fighting three actions between February 25 and March 1. During the course of the action, a PT-76 light tank knocked

Some ARVN M113s were fitted with indigenous armor kits similar to US ACAVs. In ARVN units, the vehicle commanders usually rode on top directly behind the driver rather than being stationed behind the .50-caliber machine gun. (NARA)

Armor units, regardless of nationality, normally travelled in column, changing to line formation when contact with the enemy was imminent. Here elements of an ARVN cavalry squadron deploy in 1966. (NARA)

out two M113s. Although Fire Support Base 31 was lost, the Task Force inflicted over 1,100 enemy killed and knocked out 23 tanks at the cost of 11 killed and 286 wounded.

The South Vietnamese committed additional forces, including marines, and captured Tchepone on March 6, following a heliborne assault. The greater-than-expected strength of the enemy force and supply and transport problems caused by high helicopter losses – over 108 were destroyed and 600 damaged – prompted the South Vietnamese to begin withdrawal planning almost immediately after the capture of Tchepone. Morale began to suffer due to supply difficulties. As the withdrawal began in earnest, the fire support bases started to fall to the enemy and the departure took on the

The result of an antitank mine explosion. The NVA and VC quickly learned to offset the mines' triggering devices or detonate them on command so that they exploded under the hull where they caused the greatest damage rather than under the tracks. Units initially responded by lining the hull floor with sandbags, but both the US and Australia developed belly armor kits. The US kit only protected the forward one-third of the vehicle, leaving the passenger compartment vulnerable. (NARA)

Enemy weapons and tactics ...

Initially surprised by the M113s and their maneuverability and firepower, the VC and the NVA quickly developed means to attack them. Mines, both pressure- and command-detonated, were the cause of most armored vehicle casualties. They were commonly used on roads, trails used by armored vehicles, and in areas where the terrain would channel armored vehicle movement into predictable areas. Even after "jungle busting" new trails en route to an objective, units quickly learned not to return using the same path because the enemy would slip in behind the unit in order to plant mines in the newly created trail. The VC and NVA learned to increase the lethality of mines by using offset triggering devices that allowed mines to explode under the hull, rather than tracks, where they did the greatest damage. The M113 was particularly vulnerable to large antitank mines; a mine that would merely disable a tank could completely destroy an M113, killing or wounding the entire crew. The enemy also fielded increasing numbers of more potent weapons. The Chinese Type 36 57mm and Type 56 75mm and the Soviet B-10 82mm recoilless rifles were light and easy to carry and could easily penetrate the M113's armor. They would be joined by the RPG-2 and RPG-7 rocket-propelled grenade (RPG) launchers.

... and friendly countermeasures

The standard tactics in the deliberate attack – an approach in column followed by deployment into line formation – served the South Vietnamese, US, and Australian forces well. However, the enemy's tactics and weapons quickly prompted the adoption of tactical and physical defensive countermeasures.

The earliest to be adopted was armor protection for the exposed .50-caliber machine-gunner and, later, for the side-mounted machine guns as well. Both the US and Australians developed armor kits for their M113s to attenuate the effects of mine blasts, and some units added a layer of sandbags on the vehicle floor to provide additional protection. The threat of mines also led to passengers often riding on top, rather than within, the M113. Some M113 drivers went so far as to weld extensions to their steering levers to enable them to control the vehicle while sitting on top. Ambushes were established and patrols cruised along roads at night in the hope of catching the enemy in the process of laying mines. Various detection measures and a tank-mounted mine roller were also used, but mines remained a significant problem throughout the war. In order to combat the threat of RPGs, M113s and other vehicles would carry a section of chain link fencing, which a crew would erect in front of their vehicle while in a defensive position.

The 11th Armored Cavalry Regiment (ACR) pioneered the use of the herringbone formation, in which alternate armored vehicles in column would pivot to the left and right when caught in an ambush, while directing the maximum volume of firepower on the enemy. The ACAVs had enough ammunition for about ten minutes of firing. The herringbone formation would also be adopted proactively as a defensive measure when moving through dangerous areas, each element in a column successively adopting the posture as it moved by bounds.

characteristics of a rout. Enemy pressure increased dramatically and virtually all the South Vietnamese units were under attack by March 19 and suffering heavy casualties. In a single ambush, the 1st Armored Brigade lost four M41s and 13 M113s, effectively blocking Route 9. Other units were forced to cut new trails through the jungle to escape. On March 23 the last ARVN armored vehicles left Laos.

The 45-day campaign inflicted heavy casualties: 14,500–20,000 killed and 106 tanks and about 170,000 tons of supplies destroyed. South Vietnamese losses were about 7,700 killed, wounded, or missing. Also lost were 54 M41s and 87 other armored vehicles, mostly M113s, almost all during the withdrawal.

Damage from RPG (left) and recoilless rifle (right) hits. Although its ability to penetrate armor wasn't as great as that of an RPG, the recoilless rifle's larger warhead meant that it often inflicted greater damage on the thinly armored M113s. (NARA)

E   M113 ACAV

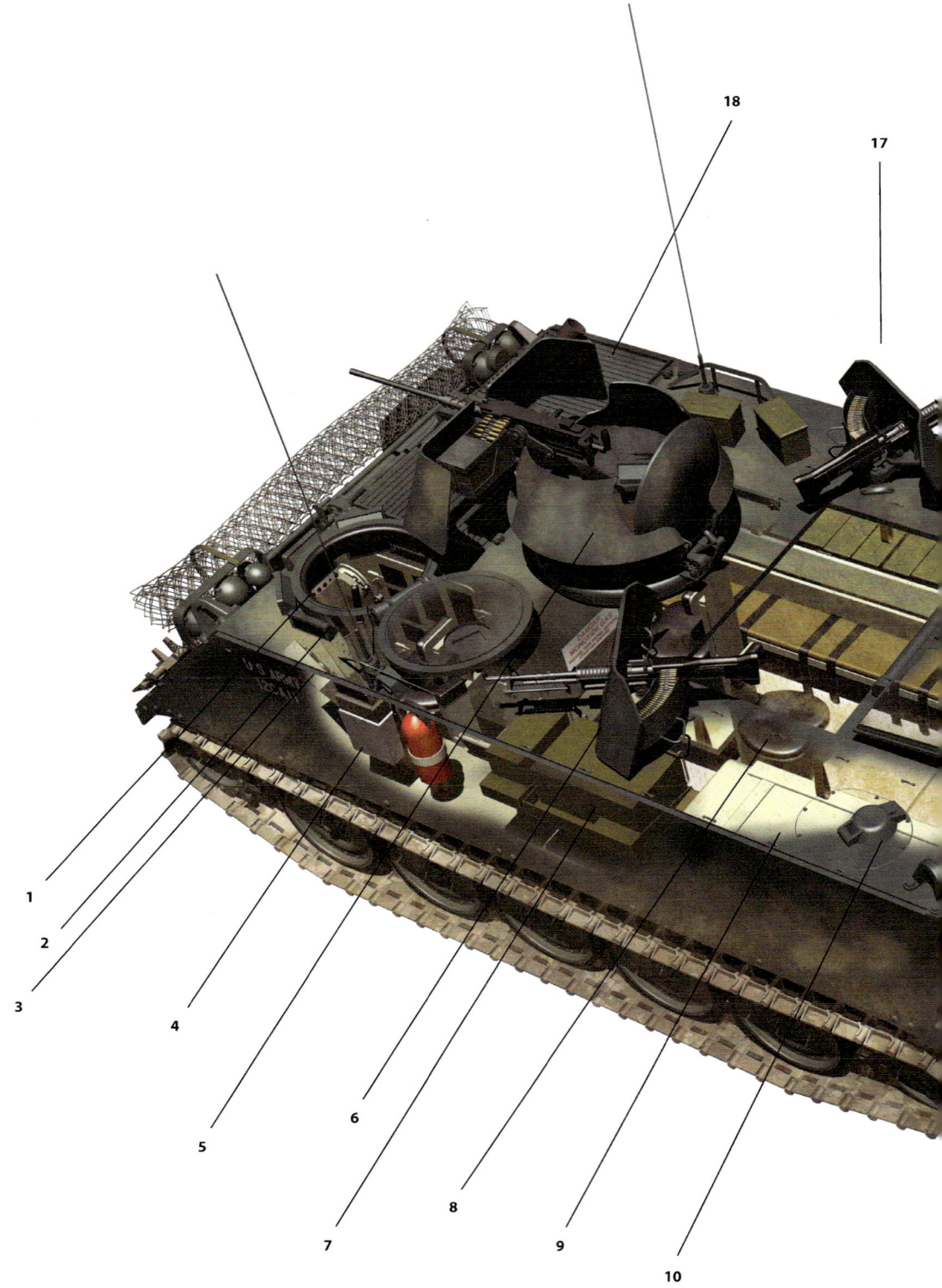

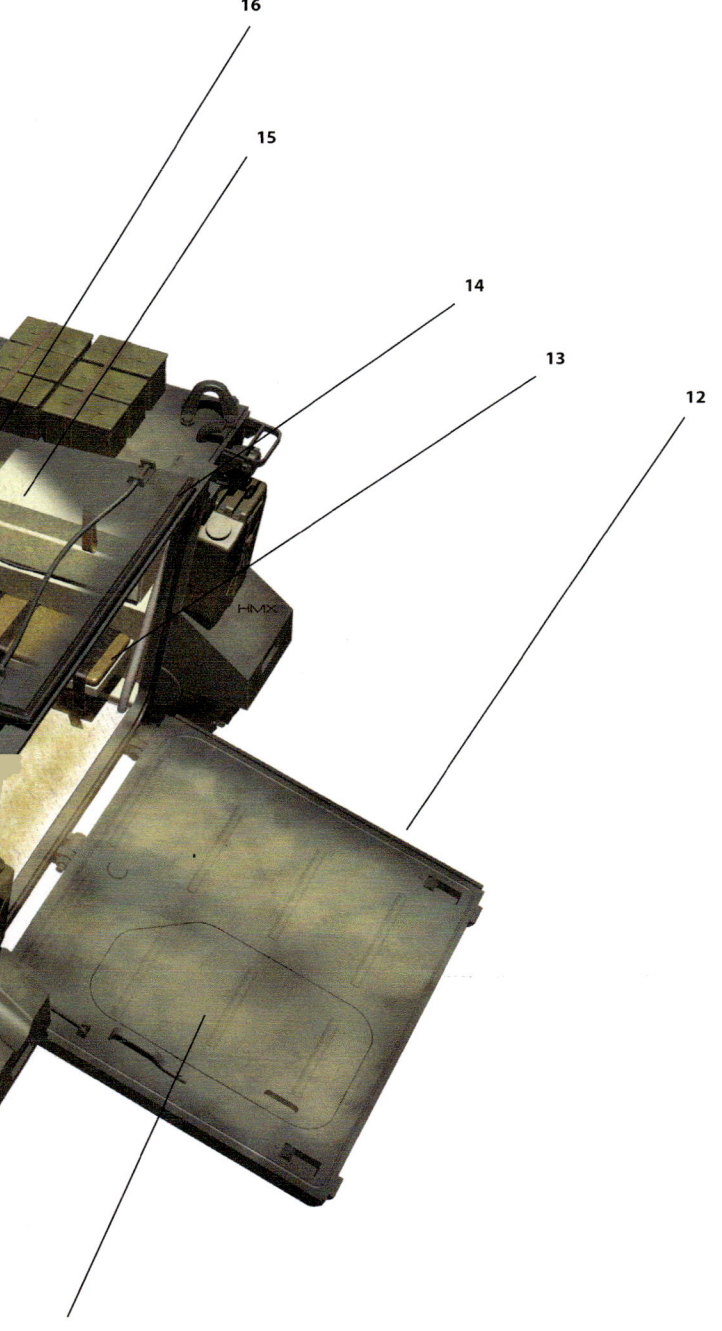

KEY

1. Driver's warning light panel
2. Steering levers
3. Driver's instrument panel
4. Periscope storage
5. Commander's cupola and M2 .50-caliber machine gun
6. M60 7.62mm machine gun
7. Radio
8. Passenger jump seat
9. Fuel tank
10. Fuel filler cap
11. Ramp door
12. Ramp
13. Passenger bench seat
14. Passenger compartment hatch
15. Battery compartment
16. Mount base for M60 7.62mm machinegun
17. M60 7.62mm machine gun
18. Engine air intake

COMBAT HISTORY: UNITED STATES

The US Army was slow to appreciate the potential value of armor in Vietnam, despite its demonstrated usefulness in the Pacific theater during World War II. A doctrinal focus on conventional military operations in Europe led to a relative neglect of thought about the use of armor in other environments. In addition, neither the nature of counterinsurgency operations nor the terrain in Vietnam was seen as suitable for armor. In fact, armor could operate with relative ease in large areas of Vietnam and even the most dense vegetation could be penetrated, albeit slowly, by tanks. The wet season and areas of soft ground such as flooded rice paddies were a bigger concern, but as the South Vietnamese had already demonstrated, the M113 was able to overcome inhospitable terrain and go places heavier vehicles could not.

A superficial understanding of the French experience with armor in Indochina reinforced the faulty notions that were prevalent in the US Army. Many of the French armored vehicles in service, such as halftracks and armored cars, had poor cross-country performance and the accompanying infantry was often carried by truck. This effectively tied many mobile operations to the road network, where they were easy prey. However, the French also had the M29C Weasel and Landing Vehicle Tracked (LVT), which had much higher mobility and enabled wide-ranging operations into areas that would have been otherwise inaccessible to mechanized forces.

Finally, and especially in the early days of the US involvement, political limits on the numbers of US forces deployed argued against sending armored units, which had a relatively large logistical "tail."

As the military situation deteriorated, it became clear that a greater US ground force commitment was required. The first US M113s arrived in Vietnam in 1965 with the deployment of the 1st Infantry Division, which had been stripped of all its armor except for the Division's cavalry squadron, the 1st Squadron/4th Cavalry.

Largely due to the insistence of its commander, the 25th Infantry Division was able to bring its armor when it deployed in early 1966 and conducted Operation *Circle Pines*. This search and destroy operation took place in the Phu Hoa Dong–Ho Bo Woods area about 20km (12 miles) north of the division's base at Chu Chi and employed one armored and two infantry battalions, one of which was mechanized. Although numerous vehicles were damaged – 11 M113s and one M577 were damaged, and one M106 from the 1st Battalion (Mech)/5th Infantry was destroyed, almost all by mines – the operation was executed successfully. More significantly, it led General William Westmoreland, commander of US forces in Vietnam, to reconsider his opposition to the use of armor and to request the deployment of the 11th ACR and other armored units.

An ACAV from 1st Squadron, 10th Cavalry, 4th Infantry Division sits behind a section of chain-link fencing designed to protect against RPGs. The crew has also erected a canopy using engineer stakes to shade themselves from the sun. (NARA)

While such large, multi-battalion armor operations did occasionally take place, the demand for armored vehicles often meant that M113s and other armor were parceled out and actions frequently involved relatively small numbers of armored vehicles. They performed a wide variety of roles including convoy security, guarding fixed installations, and serving as reaction and assault forces. Their

A common mission was the protection of land-clearing teams. Here M113s of the 1st Battalion/16th Infantry, 2nd Infantry Division provide security while Rome plows conduct operations. (NARA)

mobility and firepower were frequently decisive in regaining the initiative over enemy forces that often possessed a local superiority of numbers.

Ap Bau Bang – November 11, 1965 and March 19–20, 1967

Two major actions occurred in the immediate vicinity of Ap Bau Bang. The first took place after an infantry battalion task force of the 1st Infantry Division was ordered to provide security along a 13km (8-mile) stretch of Highway 13 in order to facilitate the passage of an ARVN regiment. The Task Force divided the area into three sectors. The middle of these contained the Task Force's command group, reconnaissance platoon, and one infantry company – A Company – as well as an attached 105mm artillery battery and A Troop of the Division's cavalry squadron. The Troop was without its M48 tanks, as they had been restricted to the Squadron's base at Phu Loi as a result of General Westmoreland's belief that the terrain was unsuitable for their use.

Following two days of uneventful sweeps and the passage of the ARVN regiment, the units occupied their night defensive positions. In the middle sector, this was in a large peanut field just south of Ap Bau Bang, and to the west of Highway 13, a north–south road which ran through the hamlet.

Just after 0600hrs on November 11, the VC's 9th Division initiated what would become the 1st Infantry Division's first major battle. The 9th Division's 272nd Regiment led the assault, supported by elements of the Division's other two regiments. Heavy weapons were positioned in and

A column of fuel trucks pause while ACAVs and M48A3s of 1st Squadron/4th Cavalry, 1st Infantry Division hand off security to the 11th Armored Cavalry Regiment. Resupply convoys were a frequent target and consequently needed to be escorted, a task for which armored cavalry units were well suited. (NARA)

near the hamlet. The infantry elements were located in the rubber trees to the south and west of the US position, while more infantry gathered to the southeast, across Highway 13. Although the first three assaults from the south and southeast nearly reached the perimeter, all three were beaten back. The first of these collapsed when the M113s charged out from their defensive position, but one of the M106s blew up after being struck by an enemy mortar round. A fourth attack about 0700hrs was launched from Ap Bau Bang to the north and reached the defensive wire. A small group of VC was able to penetrate the perimeter before this attack was also driven back, in large part by the 105mm battery using direct fire. The fifth and final attack, also from the north, faltered under the combined firepower of the armor, infantry, artillery, and fixed-wing air support. The Task Force's other two companies arrived and the VC withdrew, leaving 146 dead and numerous heavy weapons, including machine guns, mortars, and recoilless rifles, on the field. During the battle, the M113 units moved repeatedly to the most threatened sections of the perimeter and suffered one-third of the US force's total of 20 killed and 103 wounded. Two M113s and three M106s were destroyed and three more M113s were damaged.

The second battle occurred about a year and a half later. Around 1200hrs on March 19, A Troop/3rd Squadron, 5th Cavalry Regiment moved into position to defend Fire Support Base 20, occupied by a battery of 105mm howitzers. The fire support base was located 1.5km (about 1 mile) north of Ap Bau Bang in a clearing. There was a forest to the north and west and a rubber plantation to the south. Route 13 bounded the eastern side of the clearing; just beyond the road were an abandoned railway line and a wooded area.

The Troop had 20 M113s, three M106 mortar carriers, and six M48 tanks. Two platoons – 1st and 3rd – manned the customary circular defensive perimeter while the 2nd Platoon was ordered to establish a night ambush position along a trail 1.5km (about 1 mile) north of the fire support base.

The VC dominated the area and at about 2300hrs the position came under fire from a single heavy machine gun located on the railway embankment on the far side of the road. It was quickly silenced by return fire from one of the tanks and three M113s.

Shortly after midnight, the Troop again came under fire, from mortars, recoilless rifles, and RPGs. The 1st Platoon commander's ACAV was hit and

While a small number of non-standard armament configurations were fitted to the vehicle commander's station of US M113s, the most common was the M134/GAU-2A 7.62mm Minigun. Essentially a scaled-down version of the 20mm Vulcan cannon mounted on the XM163, the M134 had a prodigious rate of fire – originally 6,000 rounds per minute. From a tactical perspective, few targets required this volume of fire and the high ammunition consumption made resupply difficult. The Australians also evaluated this weapon for their M113s, but found it unsuitable for those and other reasons. (NARA)

ACAVs and M551 tanks pause during an advance through a Cambodian forest in 1970. During the advance, tanks would often lead the way, taking advantage of their thicker armor to withstand the initial onset of enemy fire and their ability to bring a high volume of fire to bear immediately during an engagement. On the left, the ACAVs face outward to provide flank protection. (NARA)

one crewman wounded, followed by a second ACAV shortly after. A third ACAV was stuck by two recoilless rifle rounds that set the vehicle on fire. Two tanks were also hit, but remained in action.

About 20 minutes later, the 273rd Viet Cong Regiment launched a massed ground assault from the south and southwest, with a secondary attack from the north and northeast, as the supporting direct and indirect fire continued against the Troop. The size of the assault prompted the Troop commander to request that the 3rd Squadron ready a reaction force to come to his aid if necessary and he was given permission to recall his 2nd Platoon from its ambush site. The main assault reached the perimeter and several of the ACAVs were swarmed by the VC, prompting them to call for small arms fire on themselves to clear the enemy. This was successful, but one burst into flames after taking a direct hit from a VC mortar round.

Due to the proximity of the VC, a portion of the perimeter was pulled in. Two more ACAVs were hit, including the 3rd Platoon commander's, in which the entire crew was wounded after being hit a second time. The 2nd Platoon arrived and was positioned to bolster the beleaguered southern half of the perimeter.

The relief force consisted of two platoons, one from C Troop 5km (3 miles) to the south and the other from B Troop 8km (5 miles) to the north. The C Troop platoon raced up Route 13 through enemy fire and reached Fire Support Base 20 at about 0130hrs. It swung west along the edge of the rubber plantation and then turned north along the forest edge, firing as it went, and then retraced its path before taking its place on the perimeter. The platoon from B Troop cleared a hasty ambush as it came down Route 13 from the north and also joined the defenders. Still in close contact with the VC, the now-reinforced A Troop was able to counterattack at about 0230hrs and expand the perimeter. The Squadron commander also arrived with his command group in two M113s. One was hit and disabled as it neared A Troop's position but was recovered and pulled inside the perimeter.

The VC launched another attack at about 0300hrs that was stopped 15m (50ft) from the perimeter. It began its final assault at 0500hrs but this was broken up by heavy air and artillery fire. The VC suffered 227 confirmed killed, while the US force had three killed and 63 wounded.

Ambush at Ap Hung Nghia – November 21, 1966

After arriving in South Vietnam, the 11th ACR established its permanent base camp just south of Xuan Loc, from which it could execute its mission of clearing and providing security for the road network in Bien Hoa, Long Khanh,

THE FIRST BATTLE OF SUOI CAT, DECEMBER 2, 1966

The 11th ACR's first major battle occurred near Suoi Cat, 50km (30 miles) east of Saigon, during Operation *Atlanta*. It took place on December 2, 1966, about two weeks following the ambush at Ap Hung Nghia. The tactics used during this action would later be adopted as the standard counter-ambush procedure within the Regiment.

B Troop was providing security at a rock quarry near Gia Ray that provided vital material for road and other construction projects. A resupply convoy, which had travelled from the rock quarry to the Regiment's base camp about 25km (15 miles) away earlier that day, was in the process of returning at about 1600hrs. The convoy's order of march consisted of a tank, followed by two ACAVs, two 2.5-ton trucks, another ACAV and a tank at the rear of the column. An armed helicopter acting as an escort accompanied it and there was also a forward air controller in a fixed-wing aircraft overhead. There was an unusual absence of civilian activity in Suoi Cat, an unmistakable sign of a likely enemy attack. Elephant grass around 1.2–1.5m (4–5ft) high grew along both sides of the road beyond the village, extending out some 60m (200ft) before merging into heavier vegetation.

Just after leaving Suoi Cat, the platoon commander, riding in the lead tank, accidentally moved his gunner override control while turning to observe the surrounding area, causing the turret to unexpectedly traverse to the right. The movement of the turret apparently caused the VC to believe that they had been detected and they prematurely detonated a mine about 10m (30ft) ahead of the tank, triggering the ambush. As both sides opened fire, the platoon leader, wounded by mine fragments, immediately radioed that he was in contact with the enemy. The bulk of the convoy was able to fight its way through the ambush, although one of the ACAVs burst into flames at the eastern edge of the kill zone after being hit four times.

Help was quick in coming. The helicopter gunship opened fire and the forward air controller requested air support. At the rock quarry just a few kilometers away, the remainder of B Troop immediately left to come to the convoy's aid. At the regimental base camp, the 1st Squadron's C Troop, D Company, and howitzer battery also left for the ambush site, followed shortly after by A Troop.

The bulk of B Troop arrived at the ambush site from the east in seven minutes, passing the convoy's burning ACAV. It moved through the kill zone under heavy enemy fire using the herringbone formation. Once it reached the western edge of the ambush site near Suoi Cat, it turned around and retraced its path through the kill zone. As B Troop was fighting its way back through the kill zone a second time, C Troop and D Company moved through Suoi Cat and followed B Troop into the kill zone, firing as they went. The howitzer battery went into firing position in the hamlet.

B Troop halted in the middle of the kill zone in a herringbone formation and allowed C Troop and D Company to continue to fight their way through. Once it was beyond the ambush site, D Company turned around, re-entered the ambush site, and took up a position adjacent to B Troop on the west. C Troop was ordered to continue southeast in order to engage enemy forces that might try to escape in that direction. By this time, A Troop had also arrived, moved through Suoi Cat, and caught a group of VC, killing 15 of them. They then took up a position in the kill zone to the east of B Troop. Enemy fire was still heavy, particularly around B Troop, but the ACAVs of A and B troops and the D Company tanks were able to deliver a volume of fire that caused the VC to break off the action.

Out of the ambushing force, a reinforced battalion of the 275th VC Regiment, over 100 enemy were confirmed dead, including four company commanders. Only one US soldier was killed and 22 wounded. In addition to the one destroyed ACAV, one tank was badly damaged.

This action served as the model for counter-ambush tactics that would be used throughout the war. The ambushed unit would use all its firepower to protect the escorted vehicles and attempt to fight its way out of the kill zone as rapidly as possible. All the available armored vehicles would then return to the kill zone to engage the enemy while reinforcements rushed to the ambush site. The herringbone formation would be used to direct a high volume of fire to both sides of the road in a bid to achieve fire superiority. Simultaneously, the maximum amount of artillery and air support would be brought to bear. The combination of the ACAV's and tank's firepower, mobility, and protection – plus the heavy application of supporting fires – was key to both limiting friendly casualties and inflicting them on the enemy.

and Phuoc Tuy Provinces. The Regiment conducted Operation *Atlanta*, its first major operation, from late October until early December. The first phase of the operation included protecting the engineers building the new camp.

On November 21 a convoy consisting of about 80 vehicles escorted by nine ACAVs (eight from C Troop and one from A Troop/1st Squadron), was moving to the camp from its staging area at Long Binh. Two ACAVs were stationed at the front and rear of the convoy and two additional pairs of ACAVs were spaced evenly throughout the convoy, the escort commander's ACAV joining the second pair. After receiving a warning of a VC presence – later identified as two battalions of the 274th VC Regiment – near Ap Hung Nghia, about 20km (12 miles) south of Xuan Loc, the escort commander alerted the rest of the convoy. At 1020hrs, the leading ACAV came under small arms fire. The first half of the convoy was able to escape the ambush zone. The escort commander's and another ACAV returned, firing at the enemy. Fired at from both sides of the road by small arms, machine guns, mortars, and recoilless rifles, a number of vehicles in the second half of the convoy were hit and came to a halt, effectively blocking the road.

Although the 45 armored cavalrymen were greatly outnumbered by the enemy force which was 500–1,000 strong, armed helicopters and fixed-wing aircraft began to arrive shortly after the ambush was triggered. Together, the helicopters and aircraft expended 42 2.75in rockets, two cluster bombs, eight 500lb bombs, eight 750lb napalm bombs, and 50,000 7.62mm and 7,200 20mm rounds of ammunition. The volume of fire caused the VC to disengage after about 30 minutes.

A relief force consisting of three different elements from 1st Squadron pursed them: the remainder of C Troop, B Troop, and the Squadron's tank unit, D Company. The main body of the VC managed to elude the relief force and the search was broken off late that afternoon. Although two ACAVs and four trucks were destroyed, there were only seven US dead. The VC suffered an estimated 100–130 killed. The firepower of the ACAV was new to the enemy and was one of the factors which prevented the ambush from achieving greater success.

The second battle of Suoi Cat – May 21, 1967

The 11th ACR's first major engagement, the first battle of Suoi Cat, (see Plate F) was a demonstration of the effectiveness of the maneuverability and firepower provided by armor. Six months later, a ten-vehicle convoy consisting mainly of the 1st Platoon, K Troop, 3rd Squadron would be ambushed by the VC in the same area, but with very different results. The VC force was estimated to be battalion size and the kill zone was over a kilometer (over half a mile) long. All but three in the convoy became casualties with 17 killed and 29 wounded.

The convoy comprised an advance guard of two ACAVs and the main body. The latter consisted of an M48A3 tank in the lead followed by the platoon leader's ACAV, a 2.5-ton truck, a jeep, and four more ACAVs. The first ACAV, belonging to the platoon sergeant, was hit by a 75mm recoilless rifle round that set the vehicle on fire and forced the crew to abandon the vehicle. The platoon sergeant and driver began to return fire. The second of the advance guard ACAVs stopped briefly to pick up the remaining three crew members from the first ACAV and continued on, fighting its way through the ambush.

An M113 with the early angular Okinawa-style armor kit for the vehicle commander. Here troops climb aboard prior to an operation. (NARA)

Simultaneously, the main body also came under heavy recoilless rifle, rocket-propelled grenade, mortar, and small arms fire. The M48A3 was hit by a recoilless rifle shell and fired a single 90mm round in return before being hit several more times and coming to a stop. It remained in action despite being hit at least 14 times by recoilless rifle and RPG-2 rounds that penetrated the turret twice, knocking out the coaxial and commander's machine guns and the tank's fire control optics.

The platoon leader's ACAV moved past the tank and was hit three times by recoilless rifle fire that wounded the entire crew. It continued to move through the ambush, stopping only to pick up the platoon sergeant and driver from the lead ACAV. Once out of the kill zone, they linked up with the remaining ACAV from the advance guard and both ACAVs re-entered the kill zone to continue the fight.

The 2.5-ton truck was badly shot up by small arms fire and ultimately disabled by a hit from an RPG-2. The passenger was killed and the driver badly wounded. The jeep attempted to fight through the ambush but was struck by a recoilless rifle round that killed the driver. The two passengers were thrown from the vehicle but later picked up by an ACAV.

The four trailing ACAVs suffered badly. One was hit by two RPG-2 rounds but managed to fight its way out of the kill zone. Another ACAV was hit by three recoilless rifle rounds that killed all but one of the crew members, who was wounded. A third ACAV was hit repeatedly by recoilless rifle rounds that killed the entire crew. The remaining ACAV sustained seven RPG-2 hits, but remained in action for a brief period before the driver was killed and the vehicle came to a stop. Three of its crewmembers were killed and two wounded.

As the two ACAVs returned to the kill zone, the platoon leader's vehicle was hit again by recoilless rifle fire, wounding the platoon leader and preventing him from firing his .50-caliber machine gun. The driver ran over a recoilless rifle and its crew as it was being reloaded as well as a VC attempting to cross the road. The other ACAV was hit repeatedly by RPG-2s that killed two of the occupants and disabled the engine. The remaining six crew and passengers dismounted and established a defensive position, from which they fought for about 20 minutes until the arrival of the relief force.

The anonymous battle – March 26, 1970

Operating in War Zone C adjacent to the Cambodian border, A Troop/1st Squadron, 11th ACR had been paired with a non-mechanized infantry unit, A Company/2nd Battalion/8th Cavalry, part of the 1st Cavalry Division. Together, they were known informally as Team Alpha. A Troop's operational combat vehicles were six M551 Sheridan tanks, 21 ACAVs, and three M106 mortar carriers.

During the night of March 25, 1970 A Troop deployed in a circular night defensive position with its mortar carriers and administrative vehicles in the center. As the mortars were conducting a fire mission, a defective round exploded inside one of the M106s, destroying it. The resulting fire involved one of the other adjacent M106s as well.

The following day, when the three combined cavalry-infantry platoons conducted separate patrols, it became evident that another 8th Cavalry unit, C Company/2nd Battalion, had run into a semicircular bunker complex occupied by a reinforced battalion of the 272nd NVA Regiment. Badly outnumbered, C Company was quickly in difficulty. Casualties began to mount, ammunition was running low, and the Company was in danger of being encircled and destroyed. Due to the lack of suitable landing zones and the proximity of the NVA, the Company could neither be exfiltrated nor reinforced by helicopter.

As it was only about 5km (3 miles) away, Team Alpha was directed to respond. One platoon, already patrolling in the direction of C Company, was ordered to continue on, while the other two platoons were recalled to the night defensive position where they joined Team Alpha's command section before moving to join the platoon already en route. They formed up into three columns, with a cavalry platoon on the left and right and the command section and one tank in the center. The third cavalry platoon followed. A Company's infantry rode on top of the ACAVs. Although they initially made good progress, breaking a path through the jungle caused the lightweight M551s' engines to overheat and the pace slowed as the columns threaded their way around overgrown bomb craters that remained from a long-ago B-52 strike. Guided by air, the columns reached C Company, surprisingly without taking fire from the NVA.

Given the approaching darkness and the relatively small size of their force, Team Alpha opted to make a hasty attack directly into the bunker

A Marginal Terrain Assault Bridge-Launcher (MTAB-L) undergoes evaluation with the 3rd Squadron/4th Cavalry, 25th Infantry Division, one of 20 sent to Vietnam for testing in the summer of 1969. They were used mainly for crossing rice paddy canals, streams, and ditches with steep banks. The MTAB-L's hydraulically launched, Military Load Class 12 bridge could span a gap of 10m (33ft). The ACAV behind it has a roll of chain-link fence stored on the glacis to be used as an anti-RPG screen (NARA)

complex. One of the M551s, its engine spent by the stress of moving through the jungle, became immobilized and had to be abandoned. A Company dismounted to follow the armored vehicles on foot.

Five tanks and 20 ACAVs formed into line and moved forward, firing as they advanced. Progress through the jungle was slow, and with increasing casualties and only about an hour of daylight left, Team Alpha was forced to curtail its advance. An RPG struck an M551, also knocking out an ACAV beyond it. A number of vehicles that had been immobilized were repaired and the M551 immobilized with engine problems was rigged for towing. Although dangerous, the failing light made returning along the trail they had created through the jungle earlier the only practical option.

With A and C Company infantry aboard, the armor began the return march to their night defensive position. The withdrawal was largely uneventful, except that the M551 being towed was hit in the turret by recoilless rifle fire and had to be disconnected from the tank towing it. Guided by illumination rounds fired by the remaining M106 in the night defensive position, the column returned safely, having saved approximately 100 men of C Company from being wiped out.

COMBAT HISTORY: AUSTRALIA

The first M113A1s arrived in Australia in 1965. The Australian M113A1s were generally similar to the US vehicles, with differences in ventilation, insulation, and lighting. The most prominent external difference was the addition of a raised box structure on the roof of the passenger compartment hatch. This incorporated a ventilation blower and filters in lieu of the M113's standard ventilator, one of the modifications added as result of the tropical phase of the Australian selection trials.

As Australia increased its troop commitment to the war, ten of the new M113A1s – 1st Troop, A Squadron, 4/19 Prince of Wales Light Horse Regiment (later designated as 1st APC Troop) – deployed to South Vietnam in June 1965. An additional six M113A1s (three of which were reserve vehicles) and two M125A1 mortar carriers followed. Originally having a battalion attached to the US 173rd Airborne Brigade, Australia's desire to pursue its own approach to counterinsurgency operations led it to request its own area of responsibility in Phuoc Tuy Province. Australia's forces were increased accordingly and the 1st Australian Task Force (ATF) stood up in 1966. The primary ground maneuver component was two infantry battalions and the 1st APC Squadron. In addition to the M113A1 and M125A1, the Squadron was also equipped with the M577A1 and the M113A1 Fitter's vehicle. It was designated A Squadron, 3rd Cavalry Regiment in early 1967.

Like the other operators of the M113, the Australians quickly realized the vulnerability of the vehicle commander while using the standard pintle-mounted .50-caliber machine gun and fabricated simple armored shields with angled sides out of half-inch plate, very similar to those fitted to South Vietnamese M113s. Although these locally manufactured shields were effective in reducing casualties, the Australians preferred more complete protection and chose the M74C that was entering service on South Vietnamese M113s as an interim solution. The first of 19 turrets were installed in late 1966. Although effective, they were cramped, and mechanical

An M113A1 from the 3rd Cavalry Regiment and infantry from 5 RAR during Operation *Tamborine*, a search and destroy mission near Nui Dat. The vehicle commander's shield was the standard Australian pattern in Vietnam, colloquially known as "elephant ears" due to its shape. Note the crewmembers are bareheaded or wear berets, typical for Australian armor crews in Vietnam. (Australian War Memorial EKN/67/0085/VN)

failures, a shortage of spare parts, and operational losses gradually reduced their numbers until they were withdrawn from service in early 1969. The Australian Army selected a slightly modified version of the Cadillac Gage T50 turret to equip its M113A1 fleet and the first vehicles equipped with the turret arrived in August of 1968. The turret could mount either two .30-caliber or a combination of one .50- and one .30-caliber machine guns, the latter configuration being highly preferred for operational reasons. The T50 also had problems. Traverse was slow, loading and operating the .50-caliber machine gun in the small turret was problematic, and the turret's sight was unreliable to the point of being useless. Eventually, it became standard practice to remove the .30-caliber machine gun from the turret and move it to a pintle mount on the top of the turret.

As the US experienced, the Australian M113A1s were very vulnerable to mines. In one 15-month period, the Australians suffered 25 damaged with ten hulls being ruptured. They believed the US belly armor kit provided insufficient protection and devised a simple folded aluminum plate that was installed under each sponson in the location of the first three road wheels. It was designed primarily to provide structural reinforcement of the hull weld, which was prone to fracture under the force of a mine blast, rather than provide ballistic protection. Installation was completed by the end of 1969. In 1970, a kit was introduced that added 38mm of aluminum armor to the entire bottom of the hull, a modification that drastically reduced crew and passenger casualties even from large mines.

While they performed many of the same tasks as their US counterparts, one unusual task for Australian M113A1s involved the movement of artillery. The range of the L5 105mm pack howitzers was relatively short and the area that they could cover from the 1st ATF base was limited, a fact well known to the enemy. In order to extend their coverage and achieve surprise, L5 howitzers were carried inside the M113A1 passenger compartment with the crews riding on top to a temporary battery position some distance from

Nui Dat. When the L5s were later replaced with M2A2 105mm howitzers, the M113A1s were used to transport them as well on similar missions, but the M2A2s' larger size meant that they had to be towed rather than carried internally.

The M113A1 Fire Support Vehicles were introduced concurrent with a drawdown in the number of Centurion tanks. Despite the recognition that they were much more vulnerable than the tanks, they performed a number of the same tasks, including patrolling, fire support base defense, protection of land-clearing teams, and the destruction of enemy bunkers during assaults, such as in the case of Operation *Iron Fox*, the assault against a heavy-bunkered base camp in late July/early August 1971.

Eight were sent to South Vietnam and six assigned to A Squadron, 3rd Cavalry Regiment. They were organized into three reconnaissance troops, each with two Fire Support Vehicles and two or three M113A1s. They were among the last armored vehicles to be withdrawn when the Australians departed.

The battle of Long Tan – August 18, 1966

Long Tan was one of Australia's largest actions and the single most costly battle in Vietnam. Although largely an infantry action, the intervention of M113A1s at the climax of the battle was instrumental in preventing the destruction of an infantry company and avoiding a major defeat that would have had significant negative operational, psychological, and political consequences.

An attack against the newly established 1st ATF base at Nui Dat, located in the heart of Phuoc Tuy Province, had been expected and the security of the base was a matter of significant concern to the Task Force commander. Intelligence sources indicated a strong VC force in the vicinity and, in the early morning hours of August 17, the base was subjected to mortar and recoilless rifle fire that caused 24 casualties and some damage to equipment, but the expected ground assault did not materialize. A patrol from B Company, 6th Battalion, Royal Australian Regiment (6 RAR) departed the base at dawn to sweep the surrounding area. It discovered the enemy firing positions and the trails made by the VC's withdrawal but didn't make contact with the main enemy force. D Company left Nui Dat in the late morning of August 18 to relieve B Company and take up the search, continuing into the Long Tan rubber plantation which it entered mid-afternoon. D Company's 11 Platoon engaged an enemy patrol and pursued it as it withdrew to the east. Unknown to D Company, it had bumped into elements of a large enemy force consisting of the main force VC 274th Regiment, an NVA battalion, and a local force VC battalion – a total of about 3,500 men.

Moving east, 11 Platoon came under heavy fire from two directions that forced it to ground. It began to sustain casualties and called in artillery support from a battery at Nui Dat. About the same time, the D Company command group and the other two platoons – 10 and 12 – which were following 11 Platoon came under mortar fire and moved to the north to avoid it. The D Company commander ordered 10 Platoon to the east to support 11 Platoon and facilitate its withdrawal. He also requested support from the entire artillery regiment at Nui Dat and reinforcements, including the B Company patrol that had not yet returned to Nui Dat. As it approached, 10 Platoon surprised a group of the enemy before coming under heavy fire from multiple directions that forced it to halt. Mounting casualties prompted the company commander to order 10 Platoon to withdraw. Meanwhile, the 11 Platoon commander was killed while adjusting artillery fire; his platoon sergeant requested additional ammunition before enemy fire disabled the platoon's radio.

Throughout the battle, heavy monsoon rain greatly reduced visibility on the ground, hampered the resupply of ammunition, and prevented close air support from attacking the enemy positions closest to the Australians.

With 10 Platoon en route back to the company headquarters position, the company commander ordered his remaining maneuver element – 12 Platoon (less one section which remained to protect the company command group which would shortly also come under attack) – to the east in order to locate the beleaguered 11 Platoon. It approached within about 200m (650ft) of 11 Platoon before it too came under fire from the northeast and southeast as the VC bypassed the isolated 11 Platoon. About a third of 12 Platoon's reduced strength of 20 men became casualties before the survivors of 11 Platoon were able to disengage and reach its position. Together, the two platoons withdrew the 300m (985ft) to the company headquarters. There the remnants of D Company, about 60 effectives, formed a circular perimeter 100m (330ft) in diameter as they fended off human wave attacks by the enemy.

Earlier at Nui Dat, the 1st APC Squadron's 3rd Troop had been ordered to the A Company, 6 RAR area in preparation for a move to reinforce D Company. However, the 1st ATF commander was concerned about reducing Nui Dat's defensive strength given intelligence reports of a second VC regiment in the area. The Task Force's other infantry battalion, 5 RAR, was just returning from operations in Binh Ba, the B Company patrol was still in the field, and only C Company was available to hold the 6 RAR lines. Consequently, the departure of the reinforcements had been delayed.

A number of the Troop's 13 M113A1s were unserviceable, reducing its complement to seven. To make up for the shortage, a section from 2nd Troop was attached, bringing the total number of M113A1s to ten, enough to transport the infantry company. The three M113A1s from 2nd Troop, however, lacked the armored shield for the commander's .50-caliber machine gun. It took about 30 minutes, much longer than usual, to load A Company. There was a further delay due to a recent change in the exit point in the defensive wire. In addition, the 6 RAR commander belatedly decided to accompany A Company on the M113A1s, so two of the APCs remained behind to load the command group, while the other eight pressed on. The movement to the Long Tan rubber plantation was complicated by the need to cross the Suoi Da Bang creek. The Troop commander was familiar with the area and knew that the only place to cross the swollen and fast-moving water obstacle was just above a small dam on the creek. Their route would take them to the southeast where, after crossing the creek, they could reach a road leading north into the plantation.

The Troop commander had been requested to wait at the crossing point for the two APCs with the 6 RAR command group. However, with nightfall approaching and knowing that D Company's situation was desperate, he decided to leave a single APC to wait for the others and continue on with his remaining seven M113A1s. The crossing was conducted with extreme difficulty. Reaching the road, he placed his own M113A1 in the center with one section of three APCs on each side, with the section commanders in the center of their sections. As the APCs advanced they made contact with a company-sized group of VC at 1805hrs moving from east to west, part of a large enemy force that had been moving to envelop D Company. Once they established that it was indeed enemy – the Troop was unsure of D Company's exact location – the Troop opened fire with their .50-caliber machine guns while continuing their advance. They dealt with a second group of VC in the same manner, killing at least 25.

On the right side of the formation, an M113A1 fitted out as an ambulance came under fire from a 57mm recoilless rifle. The first two rounds exploded against the trees nearby, shearing off the M113A1's two radio antennas. After his .50-caliber machine gun jammed, the commander ordered the driver to stop and he dismounted to engage the recoilless rifle crew, killing them and a further five enemy with his driver's submachine gun.

The troop commander paused briefly to search for another recoilless rifle team he believed to be present. Despite having command authority, the halt prompted an argument with the accompanying infantry commander, a distraction that was compounded when some of the infantry being transported took it upon themselves to dismount and advance on foot.

On the left of the formation, the three 2nd Troop M113A1s also came under heavy fire. Lacking the armor protection for the .50-caliber machine gun, two of the vehicle commanders became casualties. The troop sergeant, after crossing open ground under fire, took command of the M113A1 belonging to the most seriously wounded vehicle commander and was ordered to retire from the action in order to evacuate the commander and two wounded infantry.

At this stage, the formation became temporarily separated. Although the Troop commander and left-hand section had temporarily halted, the section on the right continued on, breaking through both the intervening enemy and the artillery fire being brought down by D Company. They actually reached D Company's defensive perimeter before turning around to rejoin the Troop. About this time, the remaining three M113A1s, including those carrying the 6 RAR's command group, had crossed the Suoi Da Bang creek and also joined the Troop.

D Company alerted the Troop that the enemy was forming up for another assault on their position that would likely overwhelm the defenders. The Troop moved north and then east. It moved cautiously in the increasing darkness toward the D Company position. Although under heavy, sustained fire, the Troop passed the D Company perimeter, driving back the enemy and crushing some of them under the APC's tracks. They swept to the east before being recalled by the 6 RAR commander to the D Company position. There the Troop disembarked A Company, which together with the M113A1s formed a defensive perimeter around D Company. After it became clear that the enemy had retreated, the D Company survivors and the casualties were loaded onto the M113A1s. The APCs moved them to the western edge of the rubber plantation and established a helicopter landing zone, using their interior lights to mark its location, so that the casualties could be evacuated.

An M113A1 fitted with the T50 turret. The .30-caliber machine gun has been removed from the turret and mounted on a pintle mount on the turret roof in order to increase space in the turret and improve its usefulness. Before this became typical, vehicle commanders often left a weapon such as an M79 grenade launcher or captured AK-47 on the top of the turret so that they could engage fleeting targets. On the roof of the hull are stored numerous boxes of machine-gun ammunition, a standard practice for Australian M113s. (Australian War Memorial P07837.046)

The next day, the APCs returned D Company to the battlefield to allow them to search for survivors from 11 Platoon – only one was found. The Troop, now reinforced by a second section from 2nd Troop, and elements

G THE BATTLE OF BINH BA, JUNE 6–7, 1969

Despite its proximity – less than 10km (6 miles) – to the 1st ATF's base at Nui Dat, the presence of a South Vietnamese Regional Force company garrison, and being the subject of Australian cordon and search operations in 1966 and 1967, the village of Binh Ba continued to harbor a low-level VC presence. On the morning of June 6, a single Centurion tank and a Centurion armored recovery vehicle (ARV) were passing the village on Highway 2 en route to Fire Support Base Virginia from Nui Dat. The Centurion was a replacement for a tank with engine problems that would be returned to Nui Dat by the ARV. As it passed the village, the Centurion came under small arms fire and was almost immediately struck by an RPG that penetrated the turret and badly wounded one of the crew. The tank commander returned fire with his machine gun as the Centurion sped off. The ARV, following some distance behind, stopped before it reached the village. It was fired at by an RPG and turned around to return to Nui Dat. The South Vietnamese District Chief sent two Regional Force platoons to investigate. As they approached the village, they came under heavy fire that indicated the VC were present in force, prompting the District Chief to request assistance from the Task Force.

The 1st ATF's Ready Reaction Force was placed on standby as soon as the attack on the Centurion and ARV became known. It consisted of a troop of four Centurion tanks, D Company, 5 RAR (reduced to about 70 men), and M113A1s from 3rd Troop, B Squadron, 3 Cavalry Regiment. By 1000hrs, they reached their holding position just south of the village. Operation *Hammer* was to be a clearing operation to destroy the enemy in Binh Ba, sweeping through the village from east to west. About 600m (about one-third of a mile) from the village the Ready Reaction Force came under fire from the nearby rubber plantation. Returning fire and continuing on, they soon came under heavy automatic weapons and RPG fire from Binh Ba itself.

One tank was assigned to each of the four streets that ran the length of the village while one M113A1 section with infantry mounted provided security on each flank. A third M113A1 section accompanied by dismounted infantry followed the tanks. Initially encountering little resistance, once past the first block of houses the enemy fire increased significantly and the tanks changed formation into two columns of two, firing canister as they advanced.

The northernmost two tanks sped through the village in order to engage a large group of VC that was attempting to escape. As they did so, one of the tanks was hit by two RPG rounds that wounded three crewmembers, two of them seriously. Exiting the village on the far side, they continued to engage the enemy and transferred the wounded from the damaged tank before abandoning it. The remaining tank then transported the wounded to where they could be evacuated by helicopter. In the southern part of the village the remaining two tanks and most of the M113A1s were hotly engaged against what appeared to be the bulk of the enemy force. Both tanks were hit by RPGs and radio communication between the tanks and APCs was lost. The combined fire from the armor and air support forced the VC to move between the houses, but the ground force was unable to maintain its advance through the village. Finally, with the tanks' ammunition almost exhausted and the Ready Reaction Force clearly facing a larger enemy force than the two platoons they originally anticipated, the Ready Reaction Force moved south and out of the village where they could rearm and regroup.

While the action was still underway, it became apparent that reinforcements would be needed. A second troop of Centurions, B Company, 5 RAR, and two sections of APCs (one a composite section that included M113A1 Fitter's vehicles) left for Binh Ba. B Company established a blocking position to the east of the village.

The second sweep of the village took place from west to east, with the tanks leading, the infantry following dismounted, and the APCs providing flank and rear security. On two occasions, an M113A1 maneuvered and engaged an enemy machine-gun team that had pinned down the infantry. Small groups of Australians would pin down the enemy in a house until a tank could fire a high explosive and canister rounds into the building, after which the infantry would clear the building room by room.

While the main enemy force – now known to include NVA as well as VC – in Binh Ba had been dislodged, the surrounding area was still not secure and further clearing operations commenced the next morning. B Company engaged a company of NVA moving in the direction of Binh Ba and an M113A1 section came under fire from RPGs. Other scattered engagements took place throughout the area. A final sweep of the village by D and B companies, the M113A1s, tanks, and South Vietnamese troops revealed the village was clear of the enemy.

of A Company cleared the battlefield and returned to Nui Dat the following day. The VC lost at least 245 killed while D Company suffered 18 killed and 24 wounded, more than a third of its strength.

Operation *Hammersley* – February–March 1970

The Long Hai hills, located about 15km (9 miles) southeast of the provincial capital of Ba Ria, were an enemy stronghold. Since 1966 several operations there had resulted in high casualties but little else. In addition to the dense vegetation, there were large numbers of bunkers and antipersonnel mines – lifted from an Australian barrier minefield that in practice served primarily to supply mines to the VC and NVA – throughout the area. The most heavily defended area was located between the two most southern of the three hill masses, the so-called Minh Dam Secret Zone.

In order to facilitate pacification efforts among the population, an effort began to improve Highway 44, which led from Ba Ria and ran along the coast south of the Long Hai hills. To provide raw materials for the project, the Australians established a quarry and nearby, Fire Support Base Isa. Fire Support Base Isa was garrisoned by C Company, 8 RAR, and a troop of Centurion tanks. An artillery battery and a section of M125A1s provided fire support. From the fire support base, patrols were conducted throughout the area.

On the evening of the 15th, a C Company platoon ambushed a group of about 100 VC, triggering an engagement that lasted over an hour and ended only with the arrival of another infantry platoon and the troop of Centurions. Thirty-four VC were killed. While this action was underway, Fire Support Base Isa came under attack, prompting 1st ATF to move the Ready Reaction Force (3rd Troop, B Squadron, 3rd Cavalry and D Company) from Nui Dat to the fire support base, followed shortly after by B Company.

While B Company occupied ambush positions, C and D companies, with tanks and M113A1s in support, conducted reconnaissance in force missions to the north and south, with the infantry riding in the APCs with the hatches closed due to the presence of antipersonnel mines both on the ground and set high in trees. There were a number of small engagements and the discovery of enemy caches. On February 18, with the Centurion troop leading and 3rd Troop's M113A1s following to provide flank and rear security, one of the M113A1s detonated an antipersonnel mine and the force was engaged by RPGs fired by a delaying party of three VC from the D445 battalion, one of whom was captured. The captured VC revealed his unit was occupying bunkers in the Minh Dam Secret Zone. Moving into the area, one of the tanks became bogged down and, while it was being recovered, the M113A1s continued the advance. With two sections in the lead, they entered the valley and immediately came under heavy fire. They returned fire while the infantry remained mounted due to the continuing danger from the antipersonnel mines that the APCs (including two M125A1s pressed into service as troop transports) detonated as they advanced. The 3rd Troop commander's APC became temporarily immobilized after it bellied on a stump. As one of the M125A1s moved to provide covering fire, it was hit by three RPGs that wounded the crew and all the passengers. The other M125A1 pulled up alongside and the vehicle commander and one of the infantry dismounted under fire and extracted the wounded passengers. By now, the tanks had arrived and one attempted to tow the damaged APC with the two wounded crewmembers inside to safety. As they did so, a VC threw a satchel charge that completely destroyed the damaged APC and killed the two crewmembers, damaged two other APCs nearby, and wounded several personnel. With the tanks' ammunition almost exhausted, the force pulled back to evacuate its casualties and resupply.

Artillery and air strikes were directed at the enemy position and B and D companies were ordered to blocking positions to prevent the enemy escaping from the valley. As B Company moved into position, it had four enemy contacts that resulted in nine wounded and four M113A1s damaged from RPG fire. A failure to notify the units of a change in plan resulted in B Company moving through D Company's position; the M113A1s mistook D Company for the enemy and opened fire, wounding ten infantry. As the C Company group again assaulted the bunker complex in the valley, it encountered only light resistance but was halted and then ordered to withdraw after the POW captured earlier told of the presence of an antitank minefield. As C Company pulled back, it was closely pursued and re-engaged by the VC. One of the tanks and one of the M113A1s were damaged by RPG fire, but the force managed to break contact with the enemy.

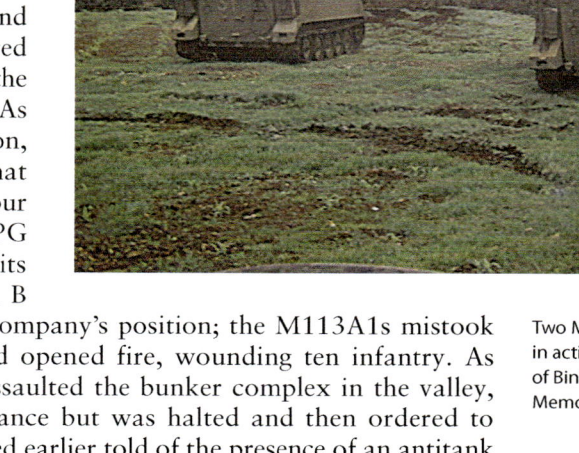

Two M113A1s from 31 Section in action during the battle of Binh Ba. (Australian War Memorial P10533.008)

Plans for coordinated battalion attack the following day were canceled in favor of a B-52 strike and the battalion withdrew to provide the prescribed 3km (1.5-mile) safety zone. The withdrawal and delays in executing the strike allowed the VC to escape. A combined ARVN and 8 RAR post-strike sweep of the area encountered no significant resistance, although nine were killed and 15 wounded in two antipersonnel mine-related incidents.

Over 100 enemy were believed to have been killed and more than 200 bunkers were destroyed. There were 70 individual and five crew-served weapons captured; 250 grenades, mortar shells, and mines; 2,000lb of food; and a large quantity of medical supplies. Official Australian losses for Operation *Hammersley* were 11 killed and 59 wounded.

OTHER FREE-WORLD FORCES

In addition to the US, Australia, and South Vietnam, several other free-world forces operated M113s in Vietnam. The potential for foreign contributions to the war effort – over 40 nations would eventually participate – was discussed as early as 1961, concurrent with discussions of the nature and scope of the US role. However, it wasn't until 1965, with the deteriorating military situation and growth in the US commitment, that the participation of other free-world combat forces began to be aggressively sought.

A Capital (Tiger) Division M113, with the colorful markings common to the Division's M113s. The vehicle shown here has improvised armor for the commander and a side-mounted machine gun. Many Capital Division M113s had the standard ACAV "A" kit, while some lacked any additional armor protection. (NARA)

South Korea

In the summer of 1965, South Korea sent an Army division to Vietnam, less one of its regiments, and the 2nd Marine Brigade. The Capital Division was located near Qui Nhon in the central highlands, a hotly contested region and key to the North Vietnamese effort to split South Vietnam geographically. The 2nd Marine Brigade was stationed near Tuy Hoa, about 80km (50 miles) to the south, another area of high enemy activity.

In April 1966, South Korea deployed another large unit, the 9th Infantry Division, in response to a South Vietnamese request. The Division's regiments were deployed near Tuy Hoa, Ninh Hoa, and Cam Ranh, enabling it to control a 200km (130-mile) stretch of coastal Highway 1 and the population centers located along it.

The South Korean forces were known for their aggressiveness and high degree of tactical competence. They participated in many operations that resulted in large numbers of enemy killed and weapons captured. Both divisions were equipped with M113s.

Thailand

The first major Thai ground contingent arrived in South Vietnam in late 1967. This unit, the Royal Thai Volunteer Regiment (nicknamed the Queen's Cobras), was collocated with and under the operational control of the US 9th Infantry Division. It included two M113 platoons, one organic to the Regiment's headquarters company and the other part of the cavalry reconnaissance troop, equipped with a total of 32 M113s.

In mid-1968 the Thai ground force contingent was expanded and the regiment was replaced with the Royal Thai Army Expeditionary Division (the Black Panthers), later designated the Royal Thai Army Volunteer Force in 1970. There were 48 M113s in the Division. Although the Thai forces were very effective, their area of operation was a relatively quiet one and there were no major actions involving the M113s.

Philippines

The Philippines' contingent in South Vietnam – the Philippine Civic Action Group, Vietnam – was focused on the construction and repair of roads and buildings, refugee resettlement, and the conduct of medical and dental aid missions. The 2,000-man force included a security battalion and was equipped with 17 M113A1s to provide local protection. An analysis of the vehicles' marking indicates they were assigned to both the group's security battalion and logistics support company.

The Philippine Civic Action Group, Vietnam's largest effort was the Thanh Dien Refugee Resettlement Project. It involved the clearing of about 4,500 hectares of forested area for agricultural use, clearing land, and building housing for 1,000 refugee families, and the construction of over 40km (25 miles) of road in the Thanh Dien forest, a Viet Cong stronghold just outside Tay Ninh City. After US and South Vietnamese forces conducted cordon and search operations to eliminate organized VC resistance, Task Force BAYANIHAN began the project. Before the project was completed in November 1965, the Task Force came under repeated attack, resulting in damage to one M113A1, an M41 tank, and several pieces of heavy construction equipment.

SELECTED BIBLIOGRAPHY

Anderson, Paul, *When the Scorpion Stings: The History of the 3rd Cavalry Regiment, Vietnam, 1965–72*, Allen and Unwin, Sydney (2002)

Cameron, Bruce, *Canister! On! Fire!: Australian Tank Operations in Vietnam*, Big Sky Publishing, Newport (2012)

Carland, John M., *Stemming the Tide: May 1965 to October 1966*, Department of the Army, Washington D.C. (2000)

Cecil, Michael, *The M113 and M113A1 Armoured Personnel Carriers in Australian Service 1962 to 1972*, Australian Military Equipment Profiles, Victoria (1994)

Dunstan, Simon, *Vietnam Tracks*, Presido Press, Novato (1982)

Hinh, Nguyen Duy, *Lam Som 719*, Department of the Army, Washington D.C. (1979)

Hopkins, Ronald N., *Australian Armour*, Australian War Memorial/Australian Government Printing Service, Canberra (1978)

Hunnicutt, Richard, *Bradley: A History of American Fighting and Support Vehicles*, Presidio Press, Novato (1999)

Keith, Philip, *Blackhorse Riders*, St Martin's Press, New York (2012)

Larsen, Stanley, and James Collins Jr, *Vietnam Studies: Allied Participation in Vietnam*, Department of the Army, Washington D.C. (1975)

Mesko, Jim, *Armor in Vietnam*, Squadron/Signal Publications, Carrollton (1982)

Rogers, Bernard W., *Cedar Falls-Junction City: A Turning Point*, Department of the Army, Washington D.C. (1989)

Starry, Donn A., *Armored Combat in Vietnam*, Arno Press, New York (1980)

Technical Manual 9-2300-257-10, Department of the Army, Washington D.C. (1968)

Tho, Tran Dinh, *The Cambodian Incursion*, Department of the Army, Washington D.C. (1979)

Toczek, David, *The Battle of Ap Bac, Vietnam*, Greenwood Press, Westport (2001)

Viet, Ha Mai, *Steel and Blood: South Vietnamese Armor and the War for Southeast Asia*, Naval Institute Press, Annapolis (2008)

INDEX

Note: locators in bold refer to plates, illustrations and captions.

3.5in rocket launchers 18
4.2-inch mortars 6, 10, **10**
20mm Gatling-type cannon 13
.30-caliber machine guns **5**, **14**, 20, **D** (20, 21), **22**, **41**
.50-caliber machine guns **5**, 5, 6, **A** (6, 7), **9**, **14**, **C** (16, 17), **18**, **22**, **41**
57mm recoilless rifles 18
60mm mortars 18
76mm cannon 15
81mm mortars 18
105mm howitzers 13, 20, 38–39
106mm recoilless rifles **B** (10, 11), 19

Ap Bac, battle of (1963) **A** (6, 7), **18**, 19–20
Ap Bau Bang (1965 & 1967) 29–31
Ap Hung Nghia, ambush at (1966) 32–34
armament
   3.5in rocket launchers 18
   4.2-inch mortars 6, 10, **10**
   20mm Gatling-type cannon 13
   .30-caliber machine guns **5**, **14**, 20, **D** (20, 21), **22**, **41**
   .50-caliber machine guns **5**, 5, 6, **A** (6, 7), **9**, **14**, **C** (16, 17), **18**, **22**, **41**
   57mm recoilless rifles 18
   60mm mortars 18
   76mm cannon 15
   81mm mortars 18
   105mm howitzers 13, 20, 38–39
   106mm recoilless rifles **B** (10, 11), 19
   M2A2 howitzers 15
   M60 machine guns 10, **D** (20, 21)
   M79 grenade launchers **41**
   M110 howitzers 13
   M134/GAU-2A 7.62mm Miniguns 30
   smoke grenades **15**, **C** (16, 17)
armor **A** (6, 7), **9**, 9–10, **15**, **18**, 20, **23**, 24, 25, **35**, **37**, **38**
ARVN (Army of the Republic of Vietnam) **B** (10, 11), **12**, 13, 18–19
   battle of Ap Bac (1963) **A** (6, 7), **18**, 19–20
   Cambodia (1970) 22–23, **31**
   Duc Co (1965) 20
   Lam Son 719 (1971) 23–25
Australia **12**, **15**, 15–16, **16**, **C** (16, 17), 37–39
   battle of Binh Ba (1969) **G** (42, 43), **45**
   battle of Long Tan (1966) 39–44
   Operation *Hammersley* (1970) 44–45
   Operation *Iron Fox* (1971) 39
   Operation *Tamborine* (1967) **38**

Binh Ba, battle of (1969) **G** (42, 43), **45**

Cadillac Gage T50 turrets **C** (16, 17), **38**, **41**
Cambodia (1970) 22–23, **31**
camouflage **B** (10, 11), **C** (16, 17), **D** (20, 21)
countermeasures 25

design and development 8–16
Duc Co (1965) 20

flamethrowers **B** (10, 11), 12, 13, **13**
formations 24, 25

grenades **15**, **C** (16, 17)

herringbone formation 25

Lam Son 719 (1971) 23–25
land mines 24, 25, 38, 44
Laos (1971) 23–25
Long Tan, battle of (1966) 39–44

M2A2 howitzers 15
M3 half-tracks 4
M44 armored utility vehicles 4, **5**
M48A3 Patton tanks **29**, 30, 34–35
M59 APC (Armored Personnel Carrier) **6**, 6
M74C turrets **A** (6, 7), 20, **D** (20, 21), **22**, 37–38
M75 APC (Armored Personnel Carrier) **5**, 5–6
M79 grenade launchers **41**
M84 APC (Armored Personnel Carrier) 6
M106 SPM (Self-Propelled Mortar Carrier) 10, **10**, **B** (10, 11), 28, 30, 36, 37
M110 howitzers 13
M113 ACAV (Armored Cavalry Assault Vehicle) 9–10, **E** (26, 27), **28**, **29**, 30–31, **31**, 34–35, 36–37
M113 APC (Armored Personnel Carrier) 4
   the ARVN in combat 18–25
   Australia in combat 37–45
   design and development **8**, 8–16
   Philippines' forces 47
   South Korean forces 46
   Thai forces 46
   the United States in combat 28–37
   variants 9–17
M113A1 APC (Armored Personnel Carrier) **9**, 9, **C** (16, 17), 37–**45**, **38**, **41**, **G** (42, 43), **45**, 47
M113A1 Fitter's vehicle 16, **C** (16, 17), 37
M113A1 FSV (Fire Support Vehicle) **15**, 15, **C** (16, 17), 39
M125 SPM (Self-Propelled Mortar Carrier) 10, 19, 37, 44
M132 flamethrower **B** (10, 11), 12, **13**
M134/GAU-2A 7.62mm Miniguns 30
M548 unarmored cargo carrier 13, **13**
M551 Sheridan tanks **31**, 36, 37
M577 TOC (Tactical Operations Center) **12**, **12**, 28, 37
markings **A** (6, 7), **C** (16, 17), **D** (20, 21), **46**
mines 24, 25, 38, 44

NVA (North Vietnamese Army), weapons and tactics 25

Okinawa-style armor kits 35
Operation *Atlanta* (1966) 34, **F** (32–33)
Operation *Cedar Falls* (1967) **13**
Operation *Circle Pines* (1966) 28
Operation *Hammersley* (1970) 44–45
Operation *Iron Fox* (1971) 39
Operation *Tamborine* (1967) **38**

Philippines, forces from the 47
PT-76 light tanks 23–24

smoke grenades **15**, **C** (16, 17)
South Korean forces 46
South Vietnam *see* ARVN (Army of the Republic of Vietnam)
Suoi Cat, First battle of (1966) **F** (32–33)
Suoi Cat, Second battle of (1967) 34–35

T13 armored utility vehicles 4
T113 *see* M113 APC (Armored Personnel Carrier)
T43E1 cargo tractors 4
tactics 25
Thailand, forces from 46
tracks **A** (6, 7), **D** (20, 21)
turrets 15
   Cadillac Gage T50 turrets **C** (16, 17), **38**, **41**
   M74C turrets **A** (6, 7), 20, **D** (20, 21), **22**, 37–38

United States 4, **A** (6, 7), **B** (10, 11), **12**, 13–14, **14**, 15, 28–29
   ambush at Ap Hung Nghia (1966) 32–34
   anonymous battle (1970) 36–37
   Ap Bau Bang (1965 & 1967) 29–31
   First battle of Suoi Cat (1966) **F** (32–33)
   Operation *Atlanta* (1966) 34, **F** (32–33)
   Operation *Cedar Falls* (1967) **13**
   Operation *Circle Pines* (1966) 28
   Second battle of Suoi Cat (1967) 34–35

VC (Viet Cong), weapons and tactics 25
Vietnam War 4, 9, 12, 13, **13**, 18–19, 28–29, 37–39
   ambush at Ap Hung Nghia (1966) 32–34
   anonymous battle (1970) 36–37
   Ap Bau Bang (1965 & 1967) 29–31
   battle of Ap Bac (1963) **A** (6, 7), **18**, 19–20
   battle of Binh Ba (1969) **G** (42, 43), **45**
   battle of Long Tan (1966) 39–44
   Duc Co (1965) 20
   First battle of Suoi Cat (1966) **F** (32–33)
   Lam Son 719 (1971) 23–25
   Operation *Atlanta* (1966) 34, **F** (32–33)
   Operation *Cedar Falls* (1967) **13**
   Operation *Circle Pines* (1966) 28
   Operation *Hammersley* (1970) 44–45
   operation in Cambodia (1970) 22–23
   Operation *Iron Fox* (1971) 39
   Operation *Tamborine* (1967) **38**
   Philippines' forces in the 47
   Second battle of Suoi Cat (1967) 34–35
   South Korean forces in the 46
   Thai forces in the 46
Vulcan Air Defense System (VADS) 13–14, **14**

Westmoreland, General William 28, 29

XM163 VADS (Vulcan Air Defense System) 13–14, **14**
XM734 Mechanized Infantry Combat Vehicle **A** (6, 7), 14, **14**
XM806E1 ARV (Armored Recovery Vehicle) 14–15, **15**